Old Testament
Bible Stories for Preschoolers
Family Nights Tool Chest

Creating Lasting Impressions for the Next Generation!

Jim Weidmann and Kirk Weaver
with Kurt Bruner

Cook Communications

For Kelly, my partner in Family Nights, and our
precious gifts from God, Madison and McKinley.
—K.W.

Chariot Victor Publishing
a division of Cook Communications Ministries, Colorado Springs, Colorado 80918
Cook Communications, Paris, Ontario
Kingsway Communcations, Eastbourne, England.

HERITAGE BUILDERS®/FAMILY NIGHT TOOL CHEST—BIBLE STORIES FOR PRESCHOOLERS™ (OLD
TESTAMENT)
© 1999 by Jim Weidmann, Kirk Weaver, and Kurt Bruner

All Scripture quotations, unless otherwise indicated, are taken from THE HOLY BIBLE, NEW
INTERNATIONAL VERSION®, NIV®. Copyright © 1973, 1978, 1984 by the International Bible
Society. Used by permission of Zondervan Publishing House. All rights reserved.

First edition 1999

Edited by Steve Parolini
Design by Bill Gray
Cover and Interior Illustrations by Guy Wolek

ISBN 1-56476-738-8

Printed and bound in the United States of America
02 01   5 4 3

Heritage Builders®/Family Night Tool Chest—Bible Stories for Preschoolers™ (Old Testament) is a
Heritage Builders® book. To contact Heritage Builders Association, send email to:
Hbuilders@aol.com.

Contents

Family Nights for Preschoolers on Old Testament Bible Stories

The Heritage Builders® Series

This resource was created as an outreach of the Heritage Builders Association—a network of families and churches committed to passing a strong heritage to the next generation. Designed to motivate and assist families as they become intentional about the heritage passing process, this series draws upon the collective wisdom of parents, grandparents, church leaders, and family life experts, in an effort to provide balanced, biblical parenting advice along with effective, practical tools for family living. For more information on the goals and work of Heritage Builders Association, please see page 105.

Kurt Bruner, M.A.
Executive Editor
Heritage Builders® Series

⊚ Introduction

There is toothpaste all over the plastic-covered table. Four young kids are having the time of their lives squeezing the paste out of the tube—trying to expunge every drop like Dad told them to. "Okay," says Dad, slapping a twenty-dollar bill onto the table. "The first person to get the toothpaste back into their tube gets this money!" Little hands begin working to shove the peppermint pile back into rolled-up tubes—with very limited success.

Jim is in the midst of a weekly routine in the Weidmann home when he and his wife spend time creating "impression points" with the kids. "We can't do it, Dad!" protests the youngest child.

"The Bible tells us that's just like your tongue. Once the words come out, it's impossible to get them back in. You need to be careful what you say because you may wish you could take it back." An unforgettable impression is made.

Impression points occur every day of our lives. Intentionally or not, we impress upon our children our values, preferences, beliefs, quirks, and concerns. It happens both through our talk and through our walk. When we do it right, we can turn them on to the things we believe. But when we do it wrong, we can turn them off to the values we most hope they will embrace. The goal is to find ways of making this reality work for us, rather than against us. How? By creating and capturing opportunities to impress upon the next generation our values and beliefs. In other words, through what we've labeled impression points.

The kids are all standing at the foot of the stairs. Jim is at the top of that same staircase. They wait eagerly for Dad's instructions.

"I'll take you to Baskin Robbins for ice cream if you can figure how to get up here." He has the attention of all four kids. "But there are a few rules. First, you can't touch the stairs. Second, you can't touch the railing. Now, begin!"

After several contemplative moments, the youngest speaks up. "That's impossible, Dad! How can we get to where you are without touching the stairs or the railing?"

After some disgruntled agreement from two of the other children, Jacob gets an idea. "Hey, Dad. Come down here." Jim walks down the stairs. "Now bend over while I get on your back. Okay, climb the stairs."

Bingo! Jim proceeds to parallel this simple game with how it is impossible to get to God on our own. But when we trust Christ's completed work on our behalf, we can get to heaven. A lasting impression is made. After a trip up the stairs on Dad's back, the whole gang piles into the minivan for a double scoop of mint-chip.

Six years ago, Jim and his wife Janet began setting aside time to intentionally impress upon the kids their values and beliefs through a weekly ritual called "family night." They play games, talk, study, and do the things which reinforce the importance of family and faith. It is during these times that they intentionally create these impression points with their kids. The impact? The kids are having fun and a heritage is being passed.

⟲ intentional or "oops"?

Sometimes, we accidentally impress the wrong things on our kids rather than intentionally impressing the right things. But there is an effective, easy way to change that. Routine family nights are a powerful tool for creating intentional impression points with our children.

The concept behind family nights is rooted in a biblical mandate summarized in Deuteronomy 6:5-9.

> *"Love the LORD your God with all your heart and with all your soul and with all your strength. These commandments that I give you today are to be upon your hearts. Impress them on your children."*
> *How?*
> *"Talk about them when you sit at home and when you walk along the road, when you lie down and when you get up. Tie them as symbols on your hands and bind them on your foreheads. Write them on the doorframes of your houses and on your gates."*

In other words, we need to take advantage of every opportunity to impress our beliefs and values in the lives of our children. A growing network of parents are discovering family nights to be a highly effective, user-friendly approach to doing just that. As one father put it , "This has changed our entire family life." And another dad, "Our investment of time and energy into family nights has more eternal value than we may ever know." Why? Because they are intentionally teaching their children at the wisdom level, the level at which the children understand and can apply eternal truths.

☺ truth is a treasure

Two boys are running all over the house, carefully following the complex and challenging instructions spelled out on the "truth treasure map" they received moments ago. An earlier map contained a few rather simple instructions that were much easier to follow. But the "false treasure box" it lead to left something to be desired. It was empty. Boo Dad! They hope for a better result with map number two.

STEP ONE:

Walk sixteen paces into the front family room.

STEP TWO:

Spin around seven times, then walk down the stairs.

STEP THREE:

Run backwards to the other side of the room.

STEP FOUR:

Try and get around Dad and climb under the table.

You get the picture. The boys are laughing at themselves, complaining to Dad, and having a ball. After twenty minutes of treasure hunting they finally reach the elusive "truth treasure box." Little hands open the lid, hoping for a better result this time around. They aren't disappointed. The box contains a nice selection of their favorite candies. Yea Dad!

"Which map was easier to follow?" Dad asks.

"The first one," comes their response.

"Which one was better?"

"The second one. It led to a true treasure," says the oldest.

"That's just like life," Dad shares, "Sometimes it's easier to follow what is false. But it is always better to seek and follow what is true."

They read from Proverbs 2 about the hidden treasure of God's truth and end their time repeating tonight's jingle—"It's best for you to seek what's true." Then they indulge themselves with a mouthful of delicious candy!

ℰ the power of family nights

The power of family nights is twofold. First, it creates a formal setting within which Dad and Mom can intentionally instill beliefs, values, or character qualities within their child. Rather than defer to the influence of peers and media, or abdicate character training to the school and church, parents create the opportunity to teach their children the things that matter most.

The second impact of family nights is perhaps even more significant than the first. Twenty to sixty minutes of formal fun and instruction can set up countless opportunities for informal reinforcement. These informal impression points do not have to be created, they just happen—at the dinner table, while driving in the car, while watching television, or any other parent/child time together. Once you have formally discussed a given family night topic, you and your children will naturally refer back to those principles during the routine dialogues of everyday life.

If the truth were known, many of us hated family devotions while growing up. We had them sporadically at best, usually whenever our parents were feeling particularly guilty. But that was fine, since the only thing worse was a trip to the dentist. Honestly, do we really think that is what God had in mind when He instructed us to teach our children? As an alternative, many parents are discovering family nights to be a wonderful complement to or replacement for family devotions as a means of passing their beliefs and values to the kids. In fact, many parents hear their kids ask at least three times per week:

"Can we have family night tonight?"

Music to Dad's and Mom's ears!

✆ Keys to Effective Family Nights

There are several keys which should be incorporated into effective family nights.

MAKE IT FUN!

Enjoy yourself, and let the kids have a ball. They may not remember everything you say, but they will always cherish the times of laughter—and so will you.

KEEP IT SIMPLE!

The minute you become sophisticated or complicated, you've missed the whole point. Don't try to create deeply profound lessons. Just try to reinforce your values and beliefs in a simple, easy-to-understand manner. Read short passages, not long, drawn-out sections of Scripture. Remember: The goal is to keep it simple.

DON'T DOMINATE!

You want to pull them into the discovery process as much as possible. If you do all the talking, you've missed the mark. Ask questions, give assignments, invite participation in every way possible. They will learn more when you involve all of their senses and emotions.

GO WITH THE FLOW!

It's fine to start with a well-defined outline, but don't kill spontaneity by becoming overly structured. If an incident or question leads you in a different direction, great! Some of the best impression opportunities are completely unplanned and unexpected.

MIX IT UP!

Don't allow yourself to get into a rut or routine. Keep the sense of excitement and anticipation through variety. Experiment to discover what works best for your family. Use books, games, videos, props, made-up stories, songs, music or music videos, or even go on a family outing.

DO IT OFTEN!

We tend to find time for the things that are really important. It is best to set aside one evening per week (the same evening if possible) for family night. Remember, repetition is the best teacher. The more impressions you can create, the more of an impact you will make.

MAKE A MEMORY!

Find ways to make the lesson stick. For example, just as advertisers create "jingles" to help us remember their products, it is helpful to create family night "jingles" to remember the main theme—such as "It's best for you to seek what's true" or "Just like air, God is there!"

USE OTHER TOOLS FROM THE HERITAGE BUILDERS TOOL CHEST!

Family night is only one exciting way for you to intentionally build a loving heritage for your family. You'll also want to use these other exciting tools from Heritage Builders.

The Family Fragrance: There are five key qualities to a healthy family fragrance, each contributing to an environment of love in the home. It's easy to remember the Fragrance Five by fitting them into an acrostic using the word "Aroma"—

A—Affection
R—Respect
O—Order
M—Merriment
A—Affirmation

Impression Points: Ways that we impress on our children our values, preferences, and concerns. We do it through our talk and our actions. We do it intentionally (through such methods as Family Nights), and we do it incidentally.

The Right Angle: The Right Angle is the standard of normal healthy living against which our children will be able to measure their atttitudes, actions, and beliefs.

Traditions: Meaningful activities which the process of passing on emotional, spiritual, and relational inheritance between generations. Family traditions can play a vital role in this process.

Please see the back of the book for information on how to receive the FREE Heritage Builders Newsletter which contains more information about these exciting tools! Also, look for the new book, *The Heritage*, available at your local Christian bookstore.

@ How to Use This Tool Chest

Summary page: For those who like the bottom line, we have provided a summary sheet at the start of each family night session. This abbreviated version of the topic briefly highlights the goal, key Scriptures, activity overview, main points, and life slogan. On the reverse side of this detachable page there is space provided for you to write down any ideas you wish to add or alter as you make the lesson your own.

Step-by-step: For those seeking suggestions and directions for each step in the family night process, we have provided a section which walks you through every activity, question, Scripture reading, and discussion point. Feel free to follow each step as written as you conduct the session, or read through this portion in preparation for your time together.

À la carte: We strongly encourage you to use the material in this book in an "à la carte" manner. In other words, pick and choose the questions, activities, Scriptures, age-appropriate ideas, etc. which best fit your family. This book is not intended to serve as a curriculum, requiring compliance with our sequence and plan, but rather as a tool chest from which you can grab what works for you and which can be altered to fit your family situation.

The long and the short of it: Each family night topic presented in this book includes several activities, related Scriptures, and possible discussion items. Do not feel it is necessary to conduct them all in a single family night. You may wish to spread one topic over several weeks using smaller portions of each chapter, depending upon the attention span of the kids and the energy level of the parents. Remember, short and effective is better than long and thorough.

Journaling: Finally, we have provided space with each session for you to capture a record of meaningful comments, funny happenings, and unplanned moments which will inevitably occur during family night. Keep a notebook of these journal entries for future reference. You will treasure this permanent record of the heritage passing process for years to come.

@ Special Notes

An abundance of resources can assist you in teaching *Bible Stories for Preschoolers (Old Testament)*. It is not necessary to *purchase* all the resources below. Consider the following:
  • Check your church library.
  • Check the church libraries of larger churches in town.
  • Ask friends.
  • Christian bookstores will sometimes rent videos.

Videos: Several series of children's videos are available to help tell Bible stories and hold their attentions. Consider:

The Greatest Adventures Videos
> *The Creation*
> *Daniel and the Lions' Den*
> *David and Goliath*
> *Jonah*
> *Joseph and His Brothers*
> *Moses*
> *Noah's Ark*
> *Samson and Delilah*

In the Beginning Videos
> *Adam and Eve*
> *Noah's Ark*
> *Abraham, the Forefather*
> *Joseph in Bondage*
> *Joseph's Triumph*
> *Moses the Egyptian*
> *Moses and Pharaoh*
> *The Exodus*
> *The Ten Commandments*
> *The Fall of Jericho*
> *David and Goliath*

Other Movies
> *The Ten Commandments*

Children's Bibles: Look through the numerous Bibles available for children and find pictures relating to the Old Testament story you are telling. Read the story as part of your Family Night.

The Tiny Tots Bible Story Book
NIV Read with Me Bible
The Children's Illustrated Bible
The Baby Bible Storybook
The Children's Discovery Bible
The Preschoolers Bible
The Lion Storyteller Bible
The Beginner's Bible

Playacting: Children enjoy playacting the Old Testament stories. Almost any story can be acted out using sheets and towels for clothing, bare feet, and mop handles for walking sticks. Playacting helps children remember and enjoy the stories.

My children will playact David and Goliath anywhere and at anytime. It is their favorite, although we did the Family Night more than a year ago. As the parent I am Goliath, and the child is David. All they need is a shoestring, small towel, piece of clothing or anything that can serve as a pretend sling. The story goes:

I AM GOLIATH OF THE PHILISTINES! WHO ARE YOU?

David of the Israelites.

I HAVE A BIG SWORD AND SHIELD TO FIGHT WITH! WHAT DO YOU HAVE?

Five stones and a sling.

FIVE STONES AND A SLING DON'T SCARE ME! I'M COMING AFTER YOU. (Step forward.)

(The child swings the pretend sling.)

AWG!! YOU GOT ME! (Fall down.)

(The child walks up to the fallen Goliath.) My God has protected me.

Simple playacting can create a lasting impression. Try it!

Kirk Weaver
Coauthor

⊙ 1: Creation

Exploring the Creation story

Scripture
• Genesis 1

ACTIVITY OVERVIEW		
Activity	Summary	Pre-Session Prep
Activity 1: In the Beginning	Act out some of the events in the Creation story.	You'll need a small tent or a sheet and rope to create a tent, Christmas lights, two buckets (one with water), a coffee can with dirt, a tape recorder and cassette, and a flashlight.
Activity 2: Clay Creations	Create animals and other things out of play dough.	You'll need play dough or clay (you can make your own using the supplied recipe), safe shaping and cutting tools, and a Bible.

Main Points:

—God created the heavens and the earth.

—God created the world, stars, plants, animals, and people.

LIFE SLOGAN: "God created all things new—earth, animals, me, and you."

Make it your own

In the space provided below, outline the flow and add any additional ideas to guide you through the process of conducting this family night.

Prayer & Praise Items

In the space provided below, list any items you wish to pray about or give praise for during this family night session.

Journal

In the space provided below, capture a record of any fun or meaningful things which happened during this family night session.

Session Tip

We intentionally have provided more material than we would expect to be used in a single "Family Night" session. You know your family's unique interests and life circumstances best, so feel free to adapt this lesson to meet your family members' needs. Remember, short and simple is better than long and comprehensive.

 WARM-UP

Open with Prayer: Begin by having a family member pray, asking God to help everyone in the family understand more about Him through this time. After prayer, review your last lesson by asking these questions:

- **What did we learn about in our last lesson?**
- **What was the Life Slogan?**
- **Have your actions changed because of what we learned? If so, how?** Encourage family members to give specific examples of how they've applied learning from the past week.

Share: Today we're going to talk about an event that is recorded in the first book of the Bible—the creation of the world.

ACTIVITY 1: In the Beginning

Point: God created the heavens and the earth.

 Supplies: You'll need a small tent or a sheet and rope to create a tent, Christmas lights, two buckets (one with water), a coffee can with dirt, a tape recorder and cassette, and a flashlight.

Activity: Set up a small tent in a room that can be darkened. If you prefer, you can use a sheet and a rope to create a tent. Hang Christmas lights on the ceiling in the room and use an extension cord so you can have one end of the cord under the tent and the plug for the lights under the tent too. (You'll be plugging the lights in as a "special effect" during this activity.) Have someone with a deep voice record the "God's Voice" section (see page 18) and place the tape recorder along with the cassette in your tent. Place the buckets inside your tent too. Place the coffee can filled with dirt just outside your tent. Ask your spouse or an older child to help you by flipping the room lights on and off at the appropriate time during the activity.

When you're all set up, ask:
- **What is the first book of the Bible?** (Genesis.)
- **What does the word Genesis mean?** (Beginning.)

Explain that you're going to imagine what it might have been like when God created the earth. Bring family members into the dark room and have them sit near the tent. Climb into the tent and begin the experience by playing the tape of God's voice, following the instructions printed in the "God's Voice" section. You may need to have a soft light in your tent so you can see all the items you will be manipulating. A low wattage colored light will work well without bringing too much light into the darkened room.

After your family has experienced the "creation of the heavens and the earth," lead them out of the darkened room. Ask family

God's Voice

Have someone with a deep voice record the following dialogue. The notes in brackets are instructions for the leader of the activity.

God: I am God. Welcome to the creation of the world. I was alive before the heavens and the earth were created. I have always been alive.

Before I created light, there was water.

[PRESS PAUSE ON TAPE RECORDER. CAREFULLY POUR WATER FROM ONE BUCKET TO ANOTHER TO MAKE THE SOUND OF RUSHING WATER]

God: Then I said, "Let there be light!" And there was light.

[PRESS PAUSE. HAVE A FAMILY MEMBER FLIP THE LIGHT SWITCH ON AND OFF A FEW TIMES, ENDING WITH THEM TURNED OFF.]

God: The darkness was called night and the light was called day. Then I created dry ground called land, and the bodies of water called seas.

[PRESS PAUSE. HAVE FAMILY MEMBERS PASS AROUND THE CAN OF DIRT TO TOUCH. POUR THE WATER FROM ONE BUCKET TO ANOTHER TO MAKE THE SOUND OF RUSHING WATER AGAIN.]

God: Then I created the sun.

[PRESS PAUSE. REACH OUTSIDE OF THE TENT AND SHINE THE FLASHLIGHT ONTO THE CEILING.]

God: Then I created the stars.

[PRESS PAUSE. PLUG IN THE CHRISTMAS LIGHTS AND LEAVE THEM ON.]

God: Now you know what it was like long ago when I created the heavens and the earth. I made the earth and everything on it for you.

[PRESS STOP. USE THE FLASHLIGHT TO LEAD FAMILY MEMBERS OUT OF THE DARK ROOM.]

members to each name one thing that God created and why they're thankful for that thing. Then close this activity with a prayer, thanking God for those things mentioned by your family members.

ACTIVITY 2: Clay Creations

Point: God created the world, stars, plants, animals, and people.

 **Supplies:** You'll need play dough or clay (you can make your own using the supplied recipe in the margin), safe shaping and cutting tools, and a Bible.

Activity: Sit around a table with family members. Give each person a supply of play dough (you can purchase this from a toy store or make your own—see the recipe in the margin).

Say: **In the first book of the Bible, Genesis, we learn about the beginning of things. We learn all about how God created plants, animals, seas, and many other things.**

Read aloud a portion of Genesis 1 to help family members learn more about the creation of the world.

Have family members use their play dough to create one or more items from the passage in Genesis. As each item is completed, place it in the center of the table for all to see. Have children explain what they created.

Then ask:
- **How did you know what shape to use to make your creation?** (I know what a star looks like; I've seen animals before.)
- **What was it like to create something using play dough?** (It was fun; I like it; it was kind of messy.)

Share: When God created all these things, He didn't have coloring books or movies to look at to know how to form them, He was the one who made up what they would look like! Just like you had fun creating, the Bible tells us that God was pleased with His creation. When we follow God, He is pleased with us.

Play Dough Recipe

INGREDIENTS:
  1 cup flour
  1 cup water
  1 tablespoon vegetable oil
  1/2 cup salt
  1 teaspoon cream of tartar
  food coloring of choice

Mix ingredients (except food coloring) in a saucepan and cook for 2 to 5 minutes on medium heat. When the dough pulls away from the side of the pan while mixing, it is done. Knead in food coloring until dough is cool. Store in air tight containers.

Place the play dough creations in a prominent place in your home as a reminder of God's creation of the world.

WRAP-UP

Gather everyone in a circle and have family members take turns answering this question: **What's one thing you've learned about God today?**

Next, tell kids you've got a new "Life Slogan" you'd like to share with them.

Life Slogan: Today's Life Slogan is this: "God created all things new— earth, animals, me, and you." Have family members repeat the slogan two or three times to help them learn it. Then encourage them to practice saying it during the week so they can talk about it at your next family night session.

Close in Prayer: Allow time for each family member to share prayer concerns and answers to prayer. Then close your time together with prayer for each concern. Thank God for listening to and caring about us.

Remember to record your prayer requests so you can refer to them in the future as you see God answering them.

Additional Resource:

Pocket Bible Stories: The World God Made (ages 4-7)

☺ 2: Noah

Exploring the story of Noah and the ark

Scripture
- Genesis 6:14-16
- Genesis 9:13, 15

ACTIVITY OVERVIEW		
Activity	Summary	Pre-Session Prep
Activity 1: Build Me an Ark	Build a small ark, discuss how big Noah's ark was, and learn about obeying God.	You'll need a large refrigerator box, markers or paints, self-adhesive paper, stuffed animals, a Bible, and a utility knife for cutting the box.
Activity 2: How Big Is an Ark?	Conduct "ark races" to learn about true size and how incredible Noah's daily job was.	You'll need a large open area (football field or park), buckets of water, cans of animal food, bags of dog food, and flags.
Activity 3: A Rainbow Promise	Create rainbows and talk about God's promises.	You'll need sheets of colored cellophane, cardboard, scissors, tape, a Bible, and a lamp or large flashlight.

Main Points:

—Noah obeyed God when he built the ark.
—God keeps His promises.

LIFE SLOGAN: "Noah built the ark God told him to, and learned that God's promise is true!"

Make it your own

In the space provided below, outline the flow and add any additional ideas to guide you through the process of conducting this family night.

Prayer & Praise Items

In the space provided below, list any items you wish to pray about or give praise for during this family night session.

Journal

In the space provided below, capture a record of any fun or meaningful things which happened during this family night session.

Session Tip

We intentionally have provided more material than we would expect to be used in a single "Family Night" session. You know your family's unique interests and life circumstances best, so feel free to adapt this lesson to meet your family members' needs. Remember, short and simple is better than long and comprehensive.

 **WARM-UP**

Open with Prayer: Begin by having a family member pray, asking God to help everyone in the family understand more about Him through this time. After prayer, review your last lesson by asking these questions:

- **What did we learn about in our last lesson?**
- **What was the Life Slogan?**
- **Have your actions changed because of what we learned? If so, how?** Encourage family members to give specific examples of how they've applied learning from the past week.

Share: Today we're going to talk about a famous man who obeyed God, and about God's promises.

ACTIVITY 1: Build Me an Ark

Point: Noah obeyed God when he built the ark.

 Supplies: You'll need a large refrigerator box, markers or paints, self-adhesive paper, stuffed animals, a Bible, and a utility knife for cutting the box.

Activity: Read the story of Noah and the ark from an appropriate-age Bible. Then explain that you're going to build your very own ark. Get out the large box and carefully cut an opening on the top and bottom of the box, discarding the cut-out sections. Cut a fold-down door on one side of the box and a small window or two on the other side. (See illustration.)

Bring out markers or paints and self-adhesive paper and have family members decorate the ark to look like a big boat. Encourage kids to make the ark as colorful as possible. (Note: If you decide to use paints, play the game in the box first

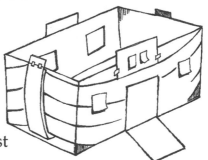

and then paint the box at the end of the evening. To paint the box first can be very messy and will create a long delay while it dries. Consider playing the game one night and painting the box another.)

Then have kids climb in and out of the box to "try it out." Collect stuffed animals (two of each kind, if possible) and have children place them inside the ark. Then have children climb into the ark too. Ask children to make their favorite animal sounds to simulate what it might have sounded like on the ark.

Then have children stand up, holding the box around them. Pretend the ark is in a rainstorm by rocking the ark back and forth while children drum their fingers on the box. For added effect, you might flash the lights on and off or use water squirters to shower your children with simulated rain drops.

After you've pretended to be in a storm for a few minutes, have kids sit down in the ark. Consider these questions:

- **How did you feel as we created an ark?** (It was fun; I liked doing it.)
- **How do you think Noah felt when he was building his ark?** (He probably wondered if it was worth all the effort; he might have felt confused; he probably enjoyed it because he was obeying God.)
- **What might it have been like for Noah and his family in the ark?** (It was probably crowded; it was probably smelly; they probably were hoping the rain would stop soon.)
- **What would have happened to Noah and his family if he hadn't obeyed God?** (He wouldn't have survived; there wouldn't be any animals; no one would be alive.)
- **What does this story tell us about obeying God?** (It's important to obey God; people who obey God will be taken care of.)

ACTIVITY 2: How Big Is an Ark?

Point: The ark is 450 feet long, 75 feet wide, and 45 feet high.

 Supplies: You'll need a large open area (a football field, though only 360 feet, or park is perfect), buckets of water, cans of animal food, bags of dog food, and flags.

Activity: Hold this family night at a football field, park, or any large open area. Take four flags and mark out an area as big as Noah's ark: 450 feet long and 75 feet wide. Older children can help you pace out the area.

Talk with the children about how the ark must have looked. Several floors full of animals. And Noah and his family were in the ark for over a year! During that time they were hard at work feeding and providing water for the animals. Organize three races which incorporate actions used in feeding the animals. (For younger children have them race the width of the ark, 75 feet, and for older children race the length, 450 feet.) Also, decide if the children are racing against each other, racing against themselves to improve their times, or working together as a team to complete the race.

Race #1: The animals are thirsty and you need to get them water. Carry buckets of water from one side of the ark to the other. The children can carry one or two buckets or for older kids use a pole across the shoulders with buckets attached to each end. The goal: get the buckets across the ark as quickly as you can without spilling water.

Race #2: The lions, tigers, and cats are hungry. Carry cans of cat food stacked in one hand as quickly as you can across the ark. Carry the cans stacked in the palm of one hand. See who can stack the most cans on one hand without dropping them.

Race #3: The wolfs and dogs are hungry. Carry sacks of dog food as quickly as you can across the ark. (If you do not have sacks of dog food, substitute bags of cut grass.)

Gather the family after the relay races, and **share: Imagine how tired Noah and his family were from feeding the animals for over 365 days! God not only saved their lives, He also gave them the strength and patience to make it through the hard times created by the Flood.**

ACTIVITY 3: A Rainbow Promise

Point: God keeps His promises.

Supplies: You'll need sheets of colored cellophane, cardboard, scissors, tape, a Bible, and a lamp or large flashlight.

Activity: Help children create a "rainbow screen." Cut a series of small rainbow-section holes in a sheet of cardboard. Then have family members each cut and tape a different color of cellophane across each of the openings in the cardboard. When the rainbow screen is complete, test it by shining a bright light (lamp or flashlight)

through the openings. You should see colored lights appearing on the other side.

Read aloud Genesis 9:13 and 15. Then **share: A covenant is a promise. God promised never to destroy the world with a flood again. And God keeps His promises.**

Shine the rainbow lights on each family member as they take turns answering the following questions:
- **What is one promise you've made to someone else?** (I promised to clean my room; I promised to obey.)
- **How easy is it to keep your promises?** (It's hard; sometimes it's easy.)

Share: God reminds us of His promise every time we see a rainbow after a storm. God wants us to keep our promises.

Shine the rainbow light on yourself as you make a promise you will always keep to your children (such as, "I promise to always love you"). Then ask family members if they want to make a promise too. If so, shine the rainbow light on them as they speak. Then close in prayer, thanking God for His promises and asking God to help you keep your promises.

WRAP-UP

Gather everyone in a circle and have family members take turns answering this question: **What's one thing you've learned about God today?**

Next, tell kids you've got a new "Life Slogan" you'd like to share with them.

Life Slogan: Today's Life Slogan is this: "Noah built the ark God told him to, and learned that God's promise is true!" Have family members repeat the slogan two or three times to help them learn it. Then encourage them to practice saying it during the week so they can talk about it at your next family night session.

Close in Prayer: Allow time for each family member to share prayer concerns and answers to prayer. Then close your time together with prayer for each concern. Thank God for listening to and caring about us.

Remember to record your prayer requests so you can refer to them in the future as you see God answering them.

Additional Resources:

Noah and the Big Boat peel and play (ages 3-8)
Noah's Ark 20-piece jigsaw puzzle (preschoolers)
Bible Greats Noah and the Ark playset (ages 4-10)
Pocket Bible Stories: Noah and the Ark (ages 4-7)
Noah's Rainy Day Gamebook (ages 4-8)
Pencil Fun Books: Noah's Ark (ages 4-7)

3: Abraham

Exploring the story of Abraham

Scripture
- Genesis 12:7-8; 13:18; 22:9
- Genesis 15:5

ACTIVITY OVERVIEW		
Activity	Summary	Pre-Session Prep
Activity 1: Remembering God	Build an altar.	You'll need bricks or large rocks, paint, and a Bible.
Activity 2: Like the Stars	View stars and imagine what Abraham might have felt about God's promise.	You'll need a large sheet of poster board, straight pins or straightened paper clips, a flashlight, and a Bible.

Main Points:

—Remember what God has done for you.

—Sometimes God surprises us with great things.

LIFE SLOGAN: "Abraham built an altar, God's promise didn't falter."

Make it your own

In the space provided below, outline the flow and add any additional ideas to guide you through the process of conducting this family night.

Prayer & Praise Items

In the space provided below, list any items you wish to pray about or give praise for during this family night session.

Journal

In the space provided below, capture a record of any fun or meaningful things which happened during this family night session.

Session Tip

We intentionally have provided more material than we would expect to be used in a single "Family Night" session. You know your family's unique interests and life circumstances best, so feel free to adapt this lesson to meet your family members' needs. Remember, short and simple is better than long and comprehensive.

 ### WARM-UP

Open with Prayer: Begin by having a family member pray, asking God to help everyone in the family understand more about Him through this time. After prayer, review your last lesson by asking these questions:

- **What did we learn about in our last lesson?**
- **What was the Life Slogan?**
- **Have your actions changed because of what we learned? If so, how?** Encourage family members to give specific examples of how they've applied learning from the past week.

Share: Today we're going to learn about how Abraham chose to worship God and about the wonderful surprise God gave him.

ACTIVITY 1: Remembering God

Point: Remember what God has done for you.

 Supplies: You'll need bricks or large rocks, paint, and a Bible.

 Activity: Read aloud Genesis 12:7-8; 13:18; 22:9, or paraphrase for your children. Explain that Abraham built an altar to remember the great things God had done for Abraham.

 Then consider these questions:

- **What are some of the things God has done for us?** (He provides for us; He protects us; He made us; He died for us.)
- **What kinds of things do we do today to help us remember the great things God has done for us?** (Go to church; pray; tell Bible stories; do family nights.)

• **Why is it important to remember the things God has done for us?** (So we don't forget God; so we always know what is right to do.)

Explain to family members that you're going to build an altar as a reminder of the great things God has done for your family. Help family members each paint their name on one of the rocks or bricks. If you have lots of rocks or bricks, paint the names of grandparents and other relatives on them or have children paint symbols representing things they're thankful for on them. Then choose a place in your home or outside where you can create the altar. Help children carefully stack the rocks or bricks to form a sturdy altar. If you like, you may even choose to build a permanent reminder by using quick-dry cement to piece the rocks or bricks together. If you do this, be sure to choose a location where the altar can remain for a long time.

When the altar is complete, form a circle around it and hold hands. Have a time of prayer, where family members thank God for the great things He's done in their lives. You may wish to visit this altar as a family on a regular basis to remind everyone of God's faithfulness.

ACTIVITY 2: Like the Stars

Point: Sometimes God surprises us with great things.

Supplies: You'll need a large sheet of poster board, straight pins or straightened paper clips, a flashlight, and a Bible.

Activity: Set a large sheet of poster board on a carpeted area in your home. If you don't have a carpeted area, set it on an old blanket or other soft surface. Give older children each a straight pin and give younger children a straightened paper clip or other item that can punch a tiny hole through the poster board. Have children carefully punch the pins and paper clips through the poster board to make as many tiny holes as they can. Encourage safety—you don't want children to poke those pins or paper clips on a sibling's hand!

When the poster board is loaded with "countless" holes, hold it up to a light or shine a flashlight through it so everyone can see the dots of light. See if anyone can quickly count the number of "stars" on the poster board. Then, if you're doing this family night on a clear evening when stars are visible, take your family outdoors for the rest of the activity. Have everyone look up at the stars and imagine how many stars there are in the sky.

Share: In Genesis, we learn about God's promise to Abraham that he will have more family members than there are stars in the sky. The only problem was, Abraham and his wife didn't have a baby. And on top of that, they were both very old and it seemed impossible for them to have a baby.

 Ask:
- **How do you think Abraham and his wife felt when God made a promise that they would have so many family members?** (Happy; worried, because they didn't have children yet; confused.)

Share: Abraham and his wife might have felt confused or sad about God's promise, because they didn't know if they could trust God. But God kept His promise and blessed Abraham with more descendants (that means sons, daughters, grandsons, granddaughters, and so on) than could be counted. God surprised Abraham and kept His promise.

Ask family members to share about times when God surprised them with great things. Ask:
- **What does it feel like to know that God can do great things?** (I feel safe; I feel happy about my future; I can expect great things from God.)
- **What can we learn from the fact that God keeps His promises?** (We can trust God; we should keep our promises too.)

WRAP-UP
Gather everyone in a circle and have family members take turns answering this question: **What's one thing you've learned about God today?**

Next, tell kids you've got a new "Life Slogan" you'd like to share with them.

Life Slogan: Today's Life Slogan is this: "Abraham built an altar, God's promise didn't falter." Have family members repeat the slogan two or three times to help them learn it. Then encourage them to practice saying it during the week so they can talk about it at your next family night session.

 Close in Prayer: Allow time for each family member to share prayer concerns and answers to prayer. Then close your time together with prayer for each concern. Thank God for listening to and caring about us.

Remember to record your prayer requests so you can refer to them in the future as you see God answering them.

4: Joseph

Exploring the story of Joseph's faith

Scripture
- Genesis 37–48
- Romans 8:28

ACTIVITY OVERVIEW		
Activity	Summary	Pre-Session Prep
Activity 1: Good and Bad	Act out good and bad things that happened to Joseph.	You'll need a Bible and a camera (optional).
Activity 2: That's Not Fair!	Compare gifts of candy and learn about jealousy.	You'll need different-size boxes of candy or other treats and a Bible.

Main Points:

—We can learn and grow from good and bad situations.

—Being jealous means wanting things other people have.

LIFE SLOGAN: "Whether times were bad or good; strong in faith, Joseph stood."

Make it your own
In the space provided below, outline the flow and add any additional ideas to guide you through the process of conducting this family night.

Prayer & Praise Items
In the space provided below, list any items you wish to pray about or give praise for during this family night session.

Journal
In the space provided below, capture a record of any fun or meaningful things which happened during this family night session.

Session Tip

We intentionally have provided more material than we would expect to be used in a single "Family Night" session. You know your family's unique interests and life circumstances best, so feel free to adapt this lesson to meet your family members' needs. Remember, short and simple is better than long and comprehensive.

 WARM-UP

Open with Prayer: Begin by having a family member pray, asking God to help everyone in the family understand more about Him through this time. After prayer, review your last lesson by asking these questions:

- **What did we learn about in our last lesson?**
- **What was the Life Slogan?**
- **Have your actions changed because of what we learned? If so, how?** Encourage family members to give specific examples of how they've applied learning from the past week.

Share: Today we're going to learn about a faithful follower of God, Joseph. We're going to discover how God is with us in good times and in bad times, and why it's important to love each other and not always want what someone else has.

ACTIVITY 1: Good and Bad

Point: We can learn and grow from good and bad situations.

Supplies: You'll need a Bible and a camera (optional).

Activity: Summarize Genesis 37–48 by telling family members about some of the good and bad things that happened to Joseph (see page 38). Then **read** aloud Genesis 45:7 and Romans 8:28.

Read aloud the following situations Joseph faced, and have children act them out after you read each one. After they've acted out a situation, have children jump up and cheer if the situation was a good one, or lie down and pretend to cry if it was a bad one. (Option: Take pictures of these scenes with camera. When the photos are developed, they will tell the story of Joseph and be a great reminder of the Family Night. It can be a lot of fun setting up the various shots.)

- Joseph's father loved him more than any of his other children.
- Joseph's brothers beat up Joseph and threw him in a well.
- Joseph's brothers sold Joseph to traders who left for Egypt.
- Joseph was sold as a slave and had to serve his master, Potiphar.
- Potiphar's wife liked Joseph and was kind to him.
- Joseph was thrown in jail.
- When Joseph explained Pharaoh's dreams, he was treated well and given a special job in Egypt.

Consider these questions:

- **What did you learn about Joseph's life from these situations?** (He had good and bad times; some bad things happened to him.)
- **What are some good and bad things that have happened to you?** (Answers will vary.)

Age Adjustments

TO HELP YOUNGER CHILDREN understand the message of this activity, use the following idea. Carefully place a small toy or candy inside a balloon, then blow up the balloon and tie it. Using the balloon, play catch with your child. Then ask "How would you feel if this balloon popped?" Then pop the balloon, allowing the treat to fall to the ground. Explain how, even though the popped balloon seemed like a bad or sad thing, a good thing happened when the candy or prize came out. Then tell younger children that sometimes things happen like that in real life—and remind them that God loves us when good and bad things happen.

Share: Joseph went through a lot of good and bad times, just like we do. But sometimes, the bad times actually worked out for good. For example, although it was bad that Joseph was sold as a slave, it was a good thing too, because Joseph was able to learn and become smart, thanks to the slave owner's great wealth. And sometimes, things that seem good really aren't so good after all. For example, even though it seems good that Potiphar's wife liked Joseph, it was also a bad thing because Potiphar became jealous and tossed Joseph into jail.

Ask family members to tell about times they thought something was bad that ended up turning out to be a positive situation. For example, someone might mention that it may seem bad when a parent yells at a child who is going after a ball in the street, but it is really a good thing because that yell might keep the child from getting hit by a car.

Close this activity by sharing how God loves us in good and bad times, and that God can use both the good and the bad to teach us and help us grow.

ACTIVITY 2: That's Not Fair!

Point: Being jealous means wanting things other people have.

Supplies: You'll need different-size boxes of candy or other treats and a Bible.

Activity: Do this activity around a dinner table. After you've completed your supper, go around and give each person his or her dessert. This could be anything from a box of candy to a bowl of ice cream. Now the trick is that you'll need to give everyone except one person a tiny amount of the treat. Give the other person a huge helping. NOTE: If you have more than one child, give the larger portion to your youngest child and the smaller portion to your other child or children.

Ask family members not to eat their dessert yet. It's likely someone will mention that "it's not fair" for someone to get more than the rest of the family members. If no one mentions the fairness of the helpings, ask children how they feel about getting less or more dessert.

Then **read** aloud or summarize Genesis 37:4-5. **Share: When Joseph's brothers saw his special coat, they became jealous. That means they thought they should have special coats instead of Joseph. And that made them hate Joseph.**

? Consider these questions:
- **How is the way some of us might feel about a person who gets a big dessert like the way Joseph's brothers felt about him?** (We also wanted what someone else had; we start to dislike someone who has something we want.)
- **When have you felt jealous about someone else?** (I wanted a shirt my friend got; I wanted to have a special toy just like my brother got.)

Age Adjustments

FOR OLDER CHILDREN, this topic will be familiar and worthy of deeper discussion. Ask your older children about the peer pressure they've felt to have things just like their friends and how that's affected their relationships with their friends. Then spend time in prayer, asking God to help them deal appropriately with their feelings about jealousy.

Share: When we want something that someone else has so badly that it makes us start to do or say mean things, that's called jealousy. God doesn't want us to be jealous, but to accept the things we've been given, whether they seem like a lot or a little.

Spend a moment in prayer, thanking God for caring for us and asking God to help us love each other and not be jealous. Then redistribute the dessert to make it seem more "fair." As you do this, explain that while life is not always fair, desserts in your home certainly can be. Then enjoy your food together.

WRAP-UP

Gather everyone in a circle and have family members take turns answering this question: **What's one thing you've learned about God today?**

Next, tell kids you've got a new "Life Slogan" you'd like to share with them.

Life Slogan: Today's Life Slogan is this: "Whether times were bad or good; strong in faith, Joseph stood." Have family members repeat the slogan two or three times to help them learn it. Then encourage them to practice saying it during the week so they can talk about it at your next family night session.

Close in Prayer: Allow time for each family member to share prayer concerns and answers to prayer. Then close your time together with prayer for each concern. Thank God for listening to and caring about us.

Remember to record your prayer requests so you can refer to them in the future as you see God answering them.

Additional Resources:

Pocket Bible Stories: Joseph and His Coat (ages 4-7)
Pencil Fun Books: Colorful Coat (ages 4-7)

@ 5: Moses

Exploring aspects of Moses' life

Scripture
- Exodus 2:1-10
- Exodus 7–12

ACTIVITY OVERVIEW		
Activity	Summary	Pre-Session Prep
Activity 1: Hide and Seek Moses	Try to find a doll representing baby Moses and learn about the meaning of Moses' name.	You'll need a doll, a basket for the doll, a towel, and a Bible.
Activity 2: Plagues	Watch as water "turns to blood" and examine the purpose for God's plagues.	You'll need a clear glass, red food coloring, water, and Bibles.

Main Points:

—God knew Moses would be found by Pharaoh's daughter.

—God used plagues to tell Pharaoh to let Moses and his people go.

LIFE SLOGAN: "God saved Moses from the river; His chosen people to deliver."

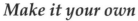

Make it your own

In the space provided below, outline the flow and add any additional ideas to guide you through the process of conducting this family night.

Prayer & Praise Items

In the space provided below, list any items you wish to pray about or give praise for during this family night session.

Journal

In the space provided below, capture a record of any fun or meaningful things which happened during this family night session.

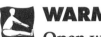 **WARM-UP**

Open with Prayer: Begin by having a family member pray, asking God to help everyone in the family understand more about Him through this time. After prayer, review your last lesson by asking these questions:

- **What did we learn about in our last lesson?**
- **What was the Life Slogan?**
- **Have your actions changed because of what we learned? If so, how?** Encourage family members to give specific examples of how they've applied learning from the past week.

Share: Today we're going to talk about two events in the life of Moses—when he was just a baby, and when he was a well-known leader in Egypt.

ACTIVITY 1: Hide and Seek Moses

Point: God knew Moses would be found by Pharaoh's daughter.

Supplies: You'll need a doll (a stuffed animal will suffice), a basket for the doll, and a towel.

Activity: Read or summarize Exodus 2:1-10. Explain that Moses' mother hid him in a basket in the river to save his life and that he was found by Pharaoh's daughter. (You may need to explain that a Pharaoh is like a king.) Then give the doll, basket, and towel to a family member. Have that person carefully place the doll in the basket, covering it with the towel. Then have the family member hide the doll. Limit the hiding places to areas associated with water (such as near a sink, in the bathtub, or outside near a pool or fountain). With fewer places to look, younger children will have more success finding the doll. When they find the doll, ask younger children how they might have felt if they were set in a basket in a river. Then explain that God was watching over baby Moses—and that God watches over them too.

 Repeat this game a few times so each person has a chance to hide the doll. Then form a circle around the doll and consider these questions:

- **What might Moses' mother have felt as she hid baby Moses in the river?** (Scared; hopeful; worried.)
- **What plans did God have for Moses that required him to be found by Pharaoh's daughter?** (He would lead his people from Egypt; God wanted Moses to be in a high position so he could help the Israelites.)

Share: Though she did not know it at the time, Moses' mother did a good thing by hiding him in the river. She trusted God to take care of him. And God did. God knew that Moses would be found by Pharaoh's daughter, and that he would some-day lead his people to freedom from slavery (you may need to explain what slavery means).

Age Adjustments

OLDER PRESCHOOLERS AND ELEMENTARY-AGE CHILDREN will enjoy a more "advanced" version of the "hide the doll" game that expands the possible hiding places. You still may wish to set boundaries such as "you can't hide the doll in a closet" or "you can hide the doll anywhere but in the basement."

ACTIVITY 2: Plagues

Point: God used plagues to tell Pharaoh to let Moses and his people go.

 Supplies: You'll need a clear glass, red food coloring, water, and Bibles.

Activity: For this activity, you'll need to prepare a glass ahead of time by placing a few drops of red food coloring into a clear glass. If possible, choose a glass with a thick base, so family members can't see the drops of red at the bottom when you show it to them.

Open this activity by **reading** from a children's Bible the story of the plagues. Explain how Moses kept asking Pharaoh to "let my people go" and how God sent a plague (you may need to define this word for your children) to show the Pharaoh how serious He was about wanting the Israelites to be free from slavery.

Then consider these questions:
- **How might you have felt if you were the Pharaoh and you**

saw all these terrible things happening around you?
(Scared; I would wonder if Moses was telling the truth; I'd be brave and not be afraid.)

• **Why did God send the plagues in the first place?**
(To scare Pharaoh; to show the Pharaoh He was serious.)

Take your prepared glass and hold it up for all to see. Then take a second glass filled with clear water, and carefully pour it into the prepared glass.

 Ask:

• **How is the way you felt as you saw this water "turn red" like the way the Pharaoh might have felt when the water turned to blood?** (He probably wondered how the trick was done; he was probably surprised too; he was sure it was a trick.)

Share: I used a trick to turn this water red, but God didn't use any tricks to fool people into thinking the water was blood—it really was! And though it took a lot of these scary things to convince the Pharaoh to let the Israelites go free, he finally gave in, recognizing God's power and the seriousness of Moses' request.

Age Adjustments

FOR OLDER CHILDREN, a trick using food coloring might not seem too impressive. However, many will be fascinated as they think about the different plagues and how each might have been considered "tricks" by the Pharaoh. Discuss with older children how they might have felt in Pharaoh's "sandals" during the plagues and the pressures he must have endured as he tried to show his power and not back down. Older children know firsthand what it feels like to be in a similar situation, and need to learn—as Pharaoh did—that sometimes you need to give in or back down.

Close this activity with a time of prayer, thanking God for being powerful and helping Moses to lead his people to freedom.

🐟 WRAP-UP

Gather everyone in a circle and have family members take turns answering this question: **What's one thing you've learned about God today?**

Next, tell kids you've got a new "Life Slogan" you'd like to share with them.

Life Slogan: Today's Life Slogan is this: "God saved Moses from the river; His chosen people to deliver." Have family members repeat the slogan two or three times to help them learn it. Then encourage them to practice saying it during the week so they can talk about it at your next family night session.

Close in Prayer: Allow time for each family member to share prayer concerns and answers to prayer. Then close your time together with prayer for each concern. Thank God for listening to and caring about us.

Remember to record your prayer requests so you can refer to them in the future as you see God answering them.

Additional Resources:

Moses Children's Discovery Bible action figure (ages 4-9)
Pocket Bible Stories: Moses and God's People (ages 4-7)
Pencil Fun Books: Baby Moses (ages 4-7)
Pencil Fun Books: Moses Leads (ages 4-7)

ꙩ 6: The ark of the covenant

Exploring the story of the ark of the covenant

Scripture
- Exodus 5:10-22; Deuteronomy 10:1-5; Joshua 3:14-17; 1 Samuel 6:12-15; 1 Kings 8; Revelation 11:19
- Exodus 25:21; 16:34; Numbers 17:10; Deuteronomy 31:26

ACTIVITY OVERVIEW		
Activity	Summary	Pre-Session Prep
Activity 1: A Different Kind of Ark	Build an "ark of the covenant" and discuss its purpose.	You'll need a large cardboard box, two broom handles, a utility knife, strong tape, gold spray paint, and a Bible.
Activity 2: Reminders of God	Learn what was in the ark and place meaningful items in their own ark.	You'll need the ark of the covenant box from Activity 1, cardboard or Styrofoam, crackers, a stick, and a Bible.

Main Points:

— God is with us.

— Remember all that God has done for you.

LIFE SLOGAN: "God gave the ark to say, 'I'm with you every day.'"

Make it your own

In the space provided below, outline the flow and add any additional ideas to guide you through the process of conducting this family night.

Prayer & Praise Items

In the space provided below, list any items you wish to pray about or give praise for during this family night session.

Journal

In the space provided below, capture a record of any fun or meaningful things which happened during this family night session.

WARM-UP

Open with Prayer: Begin by having a family member pray, asking God to help everyone in the family understand more about Him through this time. After prayer, review your last lesson by asking these questions:

- **What did we learn about in our last lesson?**
- **What was the Life Slogan?**
- **Have your actions changed because of what we learned? If so, how?** Encourage family members to give specific examples of how they've applied learning from the past week.

Share: Today we're going to talk about something called the ark of the covenant. This was a special box that held some very important things to remind people of God's presence.

ACTIVITY 1: A Different Kind of Ark

Point: God is with us.

 Supplies: You'll need a large cardboard box, two broom handles, a utility knife, strong tape, gold spray paint, and a Bible.

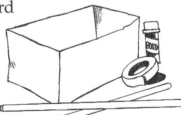

Activity: Begin this activity by describing the ark of the covenant for your family. Here are a few Scriptures to help you (you may wish to **read** a few excerpts aloud):

- Exodus 25:10-22 (Directions for making the ark of the covenant)
- Deuteronomy 10:1-5 (Moses and the ark of the covenant)
- Joshua 3:14-17 (Joshua and the ark of the covenant)
- 1 Samuel 3:3 (Samuel and the ark of the covenant)
- 2 Samuel 6:12-15 (David and the ark of the covenant)

• 1 Kings 8 (Solomon and the ark of the covenant)
• Revelation 11:19 (The ark of the covenant in heaven)

In summary, **share something like this: God gave Moses directions to build an ark—but this ark wasn't a boat, it was a special treasure box. The ark of the covenant was a symbol of God's presence and the Israelites carried it with them for many years, and even put it in a special place of honor.**

Help your children create their own ark of the covenant. Choose a large, sturdy cardboard box and carefully cut holes for the broomstick handles that will be used to carry the box. The holes need to be cut about a third of the way from the top and two or three inches from the side on each of the two long ends of the box, so the broom handles will slide through. Then have children paint the box (do this outdoors if you're using spray paint) and decorate it to look like a fancy gold treasure box. While you're building the ark, talk with your children about what it might have been like for the Israelites to build their box. Ask questions such as: **What do you think the Israelites were thinking about when they built the ark?** (That it cost a lot of money. That God liked nice things. That this box must be very special.) **How heavy might the ark have been if it was made of gold?** (Very.) **How might the people feel who had to carry it around?** (Important. Special. Tired.)

Age Adjustments

YOUNGER CHILDREN will better understand what the ark of the covenant is if they watch a video that shows how it was used. You'll find scenes with the ark of the covenant in the videos "Moses" and "Joshua and the Battle of Jericho." Or you can consider showing pictures from an illustrated children's Bible.

 When the box is complete and dry, have everyone sit around it. Consider these questions:

• **Why do you think God wanted Moses to build the ark of the covenant?** (To remind the Israelites of God's presence; so people wouldn't forget God.)
• **What are ways we're reminded of God's presence today?** (We learn about God at church; when we read the Bible we remember God; we talk to God when we pray.)

Share: The Israelites were easily fooled into following false gods during the time Moses was leading them. But the ark of the covenant became a visible reminder that God was with them, even when they felt alone or separated from God. When Jesus came to earth many

years later, He opened up the door to a personal relationship with God—so now we know God is near because He is in our hearts.

ACTIVITY 2: Reminders of God

Point: Remember all that God has done for you.

 Supplies: You'll need the ark of the covenant box from Activity 1, cardboard or Styrofoam, crackers, a stick, and a Bible.

Activity: Make cardboard or Styrofoam "tablets" to represent the Ten Commandments; find a few crackers in the pantry to represent the manna; find a small stick outside (or a popsicle stick will do) to represent Aaron's rod; and "borrow" one family member's Bible to represent the Book of the Law. Put all the objects in the ark you made in Activity 1.

Then consider this question:
- **What kinds of things would you keep in a special box like the ark of the covenant?** (Treasures; important things; things I didn't want to lose.)

Read the following Scriptures that list things in the ark of the covenant:
- Exodus 25:21 (Ten Commandment tablets)
- Exodus 16:34 (Pot of manna)
- Numbers 17:10 (Aaron's rod)
- Deuteronomy 31:26 (Book of the Law)

Share: The people of Israel kept special things in the ark to remind them of God and what God has done for them. The Ten Commandments and the Book of the Law were reminders of God's laws to live by. The pot of manna was a reminder that God provided for them (manna was bread sent from heaven to the hungry Israelite travelers). The rod of Aaron was a reminder that God kept them safe—this was the same rod (or staff) that Moses used when he approached Pharaoh about letting the Israelites go free.

 Ask:
- **What things remind you of something God has done for you?** (My clothes and food remind me that God takes care of

me; my Bible reminds me that God sent His Son, Jesus; my stuffed animal reminds me that God gives us pets to enjoy.)

Have family members each choose one or two items to place in the ark as reminders of the things God has done for them. Then have children take turns carrying the ark around the house (by holding on to the broomstick handles). After you've "traveled" for a while, set down the ark and spend time in prayer, thanking God for all the things He's done for us and asking God to constantly remind us of those things.

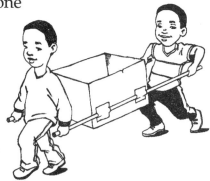

WRAP-UP

Gather everyone in a circle and have family members take turns answering this question: **What's one thing you've learned about God today?**

Next, tell kids you've got a new "Life Slogan" you'd like to share with them.

Life Slogan: Today's Life Slogan is this: "God gave the ark to say, 'I'm with you every day.'" Have family members repeat the slogan two or three times to help them learn it. Then encourage them to practice saying it during the week so they can talk about it at your next family night session.

Close in Prayer: Allow time for each family member to share prayer concerns and answers to prayer. Then close your time together with prayer for each concern. Thank God for listening to and caring about us.

Remember to record your prayer requests so you can refer to them in the future as you see God answering them.

☉ 7: Joshua

Exploring the story of Joshua and the battle of Jericho

Scripture
• Joshua 1–6

ACTIVITY OVERVIEW		
Activity	Summary	Pre-Session Prep
Activity 1: Going into Canaan	Build a huge cardboard and block wall.	You'll need a bunch of cardboard boxes, blocks, and any other items to build a large wall.
Activity 2: Let the Walls Fall Down	March around the Jericho wall and watch it fall.	You'll need musical instruments (or pots and pans with wooden spoons) and a snack.

Main Points:

   —Sometimes we face things that seem impossible.
   —God can give us strength to "knock down walls."

LIFE SLOGAN: "The walls came down at Jericho town."

Make it your own
In the space provided below, outline the flow and add any additional ideas to guide you through the process of conducting this family night.

Prayer & Praise Items
In the space provided below, list any items you wish to pray about or give praise for during this family night session.

Journal
In the space provided below, capture a record of any fun or meaningful things which happened during this family night session.

WARM-UP

Open with Prayer: Begin by having a family member pray, asking God to help everyone in the family understand more about Him through this time. After prayer, review your last lesson by asking these questions:

• **What did we learn about in our last lesson?**

• **What was the Life Slogan?**

• **Have your actions changed because of what we learned? If so, how?** Encourage family members to give specific examples of how they've applied learning from the past week.

Share: Today we're going to talk about how God used Joshua to lead the Israelites to the Promised Land.

ACTIVITY 1: Going into Canaan

Point: Sometimes we face things that seem impossible.

 Supplies: You'll need a bunch of cardboard boxes, blocks, and any other items to build a large wall.

Activity:

Share: Moses led the Israelites in search of the Promised Land for nearly 40 years. But when he died, Joshua took over as leader. Soon after he became the leader, Joshua led the Israelites to the border of the land promised to them by God, Canaan. But this land was filled with cities of people who were evil and who didn't love God. One of these cities was called Jericho.

Help your children build a large wall using boxes, blocks, furniture and any other items you can find. As you supervise the creation of this wall (which can be a freestanding wall or a small area enclosed by a wall), make sure it will be OK for the wall to come tumbling down without hurting anyone or breaking anything. Also, choose a location for the wall that allows space for people to march around it.

Take your family to a place as far away from the wall as possible (while still able to see it). Have everyone crouch down and imagine thousands of people beyond the wall in the city of Jericho.

Option: Build a house of cards on a coffeetable or semi-slick surface (sports cards or 3X5 cards can be used as well as playing cards). As part of Activity 2, you can march around the table and stamp your feet, so that the cards will fall down. Older children can be challenged to build multi-level card houses.

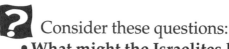 Consider these questions:
- **What might the Israelites have felt as they looked upon such a powerful-looking city?** (They'd have been scared; they'd be worried; they wouldn't know how to feel.)
- **After finally finding the Promised Land, the Israelites now had to fight those who were living there to claim that land. How would that make you feel if you were one of the Israelites—facing armies much bigger than yours?** (I'd be upset that we came so far and still had work to do; I'd be angry; I'd be scared.)

Age Adjustments

YOUNGER CHILDREN can participate in the wall-building activity if you let them place the foundation boxes or blocks. Asking them to put blocks on as the wall grows taller may be difficult and may cause some frustration if they frequently knock down the in-progress structure.

Share: Surely the Israelites—who had already been through so much—must have felt sad, worried, scared, and even frustrated when they saw cities like Jericho. But God had promised them this land many years earlier. Somehow, they had to overcome their fear to let God do things that seemed impossible.

Sometimes we face things that make us afraid too. But if God has promised to take care of us, we must trust that He will—just as the Israelites needed to trust that God would lead them to victory.

ACTIVITY 2: Let the Walls Fall Down

Point: God can give us strength to "knock down walls."

 Supplies: You'll need musical instruments (or pots and pans with wooden spoons) and a snack.

Activity: Give each family member a musical instrument. This could be anything from a harmonica to a toy drum, or simply a metal pot

with a wooden spoon. Place a snack (in a protected container) inside the wall you built in Activity 1. Then explain that God had commanded the Israelites to march around the city for six days, blowing trumpets and playing loud music. Lead your children in marching six times around the cardboard box and block wall you built in Activity 1.

Tell your family members that on the seventh day, the Israelites marched around the city seven times, playing their instruments loudly again. Do this with your family.

After marching around seven times, have children play loudly and then shout together. At this time, have family members make the wall tumble to the ground, revealing the treat you placed there earlier.

Serve the treat as you discuss the following questions with your family:
- **How might the Israelites have felt when they learned they would simply be marching around the city playing music?** (Confused; they would have laughed; they would be scared.)
- **How did God surprise the Israelites who marched around Jericho?** (He helped them to overcome the city in a silly way; they won the battle without using any weapons.)
- **How does God surprise us today? (**He gives us things when we don't expect them; He helps us when we need help; He sends friends just when we need them.)

Share: God promised the Israelites that they would someday be in the Promised Land. But when they arrived, they faced great armies and huge cities. Still, God helped them, as He helped Joshua defeat Jericho, and gave them what He promised. God still surprises us today sometimes by asking us to do hard things—then helping us to do them.

Close in prayer, thanking God for giving people strength to do great things, and for keeping His promises to the Israelites and to us, today.

Age Adjustments

OLDER CHILDREN face difficult situations often. This activity can be a great springboard into a discussion on what it feels like to face seemingly insurmountable odds at school and in all relationships. Ask older children and teenagers to tell you about times they've felt like they were facing a giant wall—and how they responded. Then spend some time in prayer, asking for God's strength to be made known in those circumstances and for God to lead them as he led Joshua to victory against all odds.

WRAP-UP

Gather everyone in a circle and have family members take turns answering this question: **What's one thing you've learned about God today?**

Next, tell kids you've got a new "Life Slogan" you'd like to share with them.

Life Slogan: Today's Life Slogan is this: "The walls came down at Jericho town." Have family members repeat the slogan two or three times to help them learn it. Then encourage them to practice saying it during the week so they can talk about it at your next family night session.

Close in Prayer: Allow time for each family member to share prayer concerns and answers to prayer. Then close your time together with prayer for each concern. Thank God for listening to and caring about us.

Remember to record your prayer requests so you can refer to them in the future as you see God answering them.

Additional Resources:

Pocket Bible Stories: Joshua and the Promised Land (ages 4-7)
Pencil Fun Books: Joshua and Jericho (ages 4-7)

@ 8: Samson

Exploring the story of Samson's great strength

Scripture
• Judges 13–16

ACTIVITY OVERVIEW		
Activity	Summary	Pre-Session Prep
Activity 1: Pillar of Strength	Dress up as Samson and topple pillars.	You'll need oversized sweatshirts, balloons, mop heads or other items to use as wigs, items you can stack to make pillars (empty boxes work well), and a Bible.
Activity 2: Fox Tail Tag	Play a game and act out stories of Samson's great strength.	You'll need strips of cloth, clothespins or strong tape, "glow sticks" or small flashlights.

Main Points:
   —God is the source of our strength.
   —God can use us in unique ways to accomplish His plans.

LIFE SLOGAN: "God made Samson strong, when his hair was long."

Make it your own
In the space provided below, outline the flow and add any additional ideas to guide you through the process of conducting this family night.

Prayer & Praise Items
In the space provided below, list any items you wish to pray about or give praise for during this family night session.

Journal
In the space provided below, capture a record of any fun or meaningful things which happened during this family night session.

WARM-UP

Open with Prayer: Begin by having a family member pray, asking God to help everyone in the family understand more about Him through this time. After prayer, review your last lesson by asking these questions:

- **What did we learn about in our last lesson?**
- **What was the Life Slogan?**
- **Have your actions changed because of what we learned? If so, how?** Encourage family members to give specific examples of how they've applied learning from the past week.

Share: Today we're going have some fun learning about Samson—a man who was given great strength by God.

ACTIVITY 1: Pillar of Strength

Point: God is the source of our strength.

 Supplies: You'll need oversized sweatshirts, balloons, mop heads or other items to use as wigs, items you can stack to make pillars (empty boxes work well), and a Bible.

 Activity: Open by telling the story of Samson and Delilah. You can use the points below or **read** Judges 16 and come up with your own summary.

Here are a few of the main points from Samson's life:

- God made Samson the strongest man on earth and he was able to do great things with his strength.
- Samson had very long hair and, because he was a chosen leader of God's people, he wasn't supposed to cut his hair.
- Delilah was a woman who tricked Samson and cut off his hair.
- When he lost his hair, Samson suddenly didn't have any strength.

- The Philistines (a powerful group of people who did not love God) captured Samson and blinded him, then threw him in prison.
- While in prison, Samson's hair grew long again and God gave him back his strength.
- Using his God-given strength, Samson pulled down the pillars of a big building, killing hundreds of Philistines. (Depending on your child, you may choose not to share the fact that Samson also died when the building toppled.)

Explain to your children that you're going to make them strong like Samson. Have each put on a large sweatshirt. Then blow up some balloons and stuff them into the shirts to make them look like muscles. Enjoy lots of laughs as you "build" your children into Samsons. Have each child wear a mop head, or some other wiglike item, to give them long hair. (Even a hand towel can be used to give the impression of long hair.)

When your "Samsons" are complete, have them show off their muscles with a few muscle poses. Have them look in the mirror, if possible, so they can enjoy the silliness. Then stack a bunch of boxes to form two pillars. Have children take turns closing their eyes or blindfold them (remember, Samson was blind when he knocked down the pillars), and let them attempt to find and knock down the pillars. Have other family members take turns pretending to be Philistines caught under the rubble.

 Then have your "Samsons" remove their costumes and discuss the following questions:
- **What was it like to pretend to knock down a building?** (It was fun; I liked it; I felt bad for the Philistines.)
- **Where did Samson get his strength?** (From his hair; from God.)
- **Where do we get our physical strength?** (From eating food; from exercise.)
- **Where do we get strength to live as God wants?** (From God; from the Bible; from going to church.)

Share: Samson's strength came from God, even though it seemed it was from having long hair. We too get our strength from God. When we follow God, He can give us the strength to do things we didn't think we could do.

ACTIVITY 2: Fox Tail Tag

Point: God can use us in unique ways to accomplish His plans.

Supplies: You'll need strips of cloth, clothespins, "glow sticks" or small flashlights.

Activity:

Share: Samson is known for unusual battles he had with the Philistines. One time, he fought and defeated 30 Philistine soldiers all by himself. Another time, Samson fought and killed 1,000 Philistine soldiers using just the jawbone of a donkey. But one of the strangest stories tells of the time Samson sent 300 foxes (with their tails on fire) racing through one of the Philistine's wheat fields. The fire spread to the whole field and eventually burnt all the crops.

Explain that you're going to play a game based on this strange story. You'll need to do this in a darkened basement (free from obstacles that could cause injury) or outdoors after dark. Attach a small flashlight or "glow stick" (they sell for about a dollar at most discount stores) to one end of a cloth strip for each family member. This cloth becomes the fox tail. Help family members each attach one tail using a clothespin or strong tape (so it will come off easily when pulled). Then turn on the flashlights (or shine a bright light on the glow stick to make them bright) and play a game of tag.

Explain that the object is to collect as many fox tails as possible without losing your own. When someone loses a tail, he or she must freeze in position and wait until the round is over (when you call "time" or when one person is left with a tail on). Play as long as family members are having fun. Then have a closing discussion.

Ask:
- **What was it like to play this game?** (It was fun; it was tiring.)
- **How is the way we all looked running around with lights on our "tails" like or unlike the way it might have been when Samson sent the foxes into the fields?** (It was probably a pretty strange sight; I'm sure the foxes weren't very happy, but we were.)
- **What do these stories about Samson's victories tell us**

about God? (God uses unique ways to get things done; that Samson was a part of God's plan.)

Share: Even though we'd never think of doing things like Samson did, we can learn one important lesson from these stories: God can use us in ways we can't even imagine in order to accomplish His will. God wanted Samson to be a part of His plan, so He gave Samson some pretty creative ways to do that. Today, God uses people in unique ways too.

 **WRAP-UP**

Gather everyone in a circle and have family members take turns answering this question: **What's one thing you've learned about God today?**

Next, tell kids you've got a new "Life Slogan" you'd like to share with them.

Life Slogan: Today's Life Slogan is this: "God made Samson strong, when his hair was long." Have family members repeat the slogan two or three times to help them learn it. Then encourage them to practice saying it during the week so they can talk about it at your next family night session.

Close in Prayer: Allow time for each family member to share prayer concerns and answers to prayer. Then close your time together with prayer for each concern. Thank God for listening to and caring about us.

Remember to record your prayer requests so you can refer to them in the future as you see God answering them.

Additional Resources:

Samson Children's Discovery Bible action figure (ages 4-9)
Pencil Fun Books: Samson, God's Man (ages 4-7)

⊚ 9: Ruth

Exploring the story of Ruth and Naomi

Scripture
• Book of Ruth

ACTIVITY OVERVIEW		
Activity	**Summary**	**Pre-Session Prep**
Activity 1: Story in a Box	Tell the story of Ruth to show how family members can encourage each other.	You'll need a shoebox, two pieces of different colored felt, and seven pipe cleaners (preferably different colors).
Activity 2: Face Magnets	Use magnets to demonstrate how family members "stick together."	You'll need a shoebox, scissors, paper or cloth, several magnets at least one inch in diameter, photos or each family member plus photos of friends and other people, and a Bible.

Main Points:
— Family members ought to be loyal to each other.
— We are a family for life, forever.

LIFE SLOGAN: "Christian families stay together, today, tomorrow, and forever."

Make it your own

In the space provided below, outline the flow and add any additional ideas to guide you through the process of conducting this family night.

Prayer & Praise Items

In the space provided below, list any items you wish to pray about or give praise for during this family night session.

Journal

In the space provided below, capture a record of any fun or meaningful things which happened during this family night session.

Session Tip

We intentionally have provided more material than we would expect to be used in a single "Family Night" session. You know your family's unique interests and life circumstances best, so feel free to adapt this lesson to meet your family members' needs. Remember, short and simple is better than long and comprehensive.

WARM-UP

Open with Prayer: Begin by having a family member pray, asking God to help everyone in the family understand more about Him through this time. After prayer, review your last lesson by asking these questions:

- **What did we learn about in our last lesson?**
- **What was the Life Slogan?**
- **Have your actions changed because of what we learned? If so, how?** Encourage family members to give specific examples of how they've applied learning from the past week.

Share: This week we're going to learn about how families are God's special plan.

ACTIVITY 1: Story in a Box

Point: Family members ought to be loyal to each other.

 Supplies: You'll need a shoebox, two pieces of different colored felt, and seven pipe cleaners (preferably different colors) to represent the seven characters in the story of Ruth.

Activity: In advance, prepare the story in a box by making seven stick figures to represent the following characters: Ruth, Naomi, Orpah, Elimelech (Naomi's husband), the two sons, and Boaz. One piece of felt will be used to represent the land of Judah and the other the land of Moab, where Naomi, Elimelech, and their two sons move to escape the famine.

Begin the Family Night by opening the shoebox and removing

the various items to retell the story from the Book of Ruth, using your own words or a children's story Bible.

- Naomi's family moved from Judah to Moab to escape a famine.
- One of Naomi's sons married Ruth.
- Naomi's husband and sons died.
- Naomi went back to Judah. Ruth went with her.
- Ruth picked up grain from the fields of Boaz.
- Boaz and Ruth fell in love and got married.
- Ruth had a son to carry on Naomi's family name.

You'll probably want to involve the children by allowing them to "play" some of the pipe cleaner characters.

When the story is completed, ask:

- **Have you ever had to move with your family? How did you feel if you did?** (Excited; sad to leave my friend; scared about what my new home would be like.)
- **Have you ever been loyal and stayed with a friend when you didn't want to or have to stay?**
- **Did you know people watch how you behave with your brother(s), sister(s), Mom, and Dad? What do you think other people see?** (A happy family; that we love each other; that we don't get along sometimes.)

Share: Ruth encouraged Naomi. When Naomi was upset, Ruth stayed with her. As family members, we need to encourage and comfort each other.

Make the point that God honored Ruth for her loyalty, because she became the great grandmother of the famous King David and it was from that family hundreds of years later that Jesus was born.

ACTIVITY 2: Face Magnets

Point: We are family for life, forever.

 Supplies: You'll need a shoebox, scissors, paper or cloth, several magnets at least one inch in diameter, photos of each family member plus photos of friends and other people, and a Bible.

Activity: In advance, take a shoebox and cut a hole in one of the narrow ends big enough to put a hand through. Tape a piece of paper or cloth inside the box to cover the hole (the purpose is to limit what the participant can see). The cloth or paper will move out of the way when a hand is inserted into the box. Buy two round magnets (at least one inch in diameter) for each child who will play the game. Glue pictures of the immediate family cut in one-inch circles on each of the magnets. Cut out additional pictures of friends and other people and put these unattached photos in the shoebox along with all the magnets photos except the one of the child who will play the game first.

To play, give the child the magnet with his or her own picture glued on one side. Tell the child to use the magnet to reach into the shoebox to see what pictures will stick. (The family member pictures will stick because they are glued on magnets.) Continue the game until each child has had a turn, and repeat as long as the fun continues.

Then **share: In Ruth 1:14, the Bible says, "Ruth clung to Naomi," in much the same way our family magnets stuck to each other. There is a special relationship between family members. Others will come and go, but we are family members for life, forever. It is important to be loyal and honor the special, loving relationship we have as family members. Even when we disagree or get upset, we need to forgive and love each other.**

WRAP-UP

Gather everyone in a circle and have family members take turns answering this question: **What's one thing you've learned about God today?**

Next, tell kids you've got a new "Life Slogan" you'd like to share with them.

Life Slogan: "Christian families stay together, today, tomorrow, and forever." Have family members repeat the slogan two or three times to help them learn it. Then encourage them to practice saying it during the week so they can talk about it at your next family night session.

Close in Prayer: Allow time for each family member to share prayer concerns and answers to prayer. Then close your time together with prayer for each concern. Thank God for listening to and caring about us.

Remember to record your prayer requests so you can refer to them in the future as you see God answering them.

@ 10: David and Goliath

Exploring the story of David and Goliath

Scripture
• 1 Samuel 17:34-40

ACTIVITY OVERVIEW		
Activity	Summary	Pre-Session Prep
Activity 1: Just a Shepherd Boy	Make a sling and protect stuffed animals from "predators."	You'll need materials to make a sling (cloth, shoe-strings), plastic golf balls or marshmallows, and stuffed animals.
Activity 2: Won't You Sling with Me?	Learn how big Goliath was and try to defeat him with their slings.	You'll need your slings from Activity 1, plastic golf balls or marshmallows, a tape measure, cardboard, markers, and a Bible.

Main Points:

—God gives us the skills we need to do what He asks of us.

—People look at outside appearances, but God looks at the heart.

LIFE SLOGAN: "David killed Goliath with a little sling; with God you can do anything."

Make it your own
In the space provided below, outline the flow and add any additional ideas to guide you through the process of conducting this family night.

Prayer & Praise Items
In the space provided below, list any items you wish to pray about or give praise for during this family night session.

Journal
In the space provided below, capture a record of any fun or meaningful things which happened during this family night session.

Session Tip

WARM-UP

Open with Prayer: Begin by having a family member pray, asking God to help everyone in the family understand more about Him through this time. After prayer, review your last lesson by asking these questions:

- **What did we learn about in our last lesson?**
- **What was the Life Slogan?**
- **Have your actions changed because of what we learned? If so, how?** Encourage family members to give specific examples of how they've applied learning from the past week.

Share: Today we're going to learn about how God used a little shepherd boy to defeat a giant—and how God looks at our hearts and not our outward appearance.

ACTIVITY 1: Just a Shepherd Boy

Point: God gives us the skills we need to do what He asks of us.

Supplies: You'll need materials to make a sling (cloth, shoestrings), plastic golf balls or marshmallows, and stuffed animals.

Activity: Begin by making a sling similar to that David might have made as a young shepherd. Cut a round piece of cloth or leather to be used as the sling pouch. Then punch or carefully cut small holes in the cloth at 2 o'clock, 4 o'clock, 8 o'clock and 10 o'clock. Lace the shoestring through the holes until ends match (see illustration). NOTE: The longer the strings, the faster the projectiles will fly, but with less accuracy.

Tell family members that David was a young shepherd boy who watched over his sheep with great care. Place the stuffed animals near your children and ask them to pretend the toys are sheep.

Share: When David was watching his sheep, he needed to be on the lookout for wild animals who might come looking for lamb chops. So David made a sling (hold up your sling) **and used it to fend off wild animals.**

Age Adjustments

YOUNGER CHILDREN will easily become frustrated if they try to use the sling. Allow them to simply throw the plastic golf balls or marshmallows at the "wild animal" during this activity. Then talk with them about how David must have practiced a lot to learn how to use the slingshot. Encourage younger children to practice things they're learning.

Give the sling to a family member and show him or her how to use it. Here's how: Wrap one side of the shoestrings around a finger and hold the other end between your fingers. Place a plastic golf ball (or marshmallow) in the pouch. Swing the pouch around. The ball will be held in place by centrifugal force. Let go of the shoestrings that are being held by the fingers and the ball (or marshmallow) will fly.

NOTE: Because this is a difficult and unpredictable action, have other family members stand far away or protect themselves while someone is trying out the sling. It's OK if children get frustrated with the sling—one of the lessons they'll learn is how difficult it was to use a sling.

Have a stuffed animal representing a lion or other wild animal "approach" the sheep. Have children take turns trying to hit the wild animal with a plastic golf ball or marshmallow launched from the sling.

After a few attempts, consider these questions:

- **How easy or difficult was it to use the sling?** (It was hard to make it go where I wanted; it was easy to use; I couldn't get it to work at all.)
- **What does this activity tell you about the young shepherd, David?** (He was good at using the sling; he was brave.)

Share: David learned to use the sling as a young boy to fight off lions and bears. God was preparing him at this young age for a much bigger challenge. God knew that someday, David would face a giant warrior named Goliath and that the skills he'd learn with the sling as a young boy would help him on that day.

- **What skill that you are learning might help you do something big someday?** (I am learning how to draw, maybe someday I'll be an artist; I'm learning to play baseball, maybe someday I'll play on a big league team.)

Share: God has big plans for each of us. We don't even know yet what He is preparing us for, but just like David, we will be called upon to use our talents to serve God.

ACTIVITY 2: Won't You Sling with Me?

Point: People look at outside appearances, but God looks at the heart.

 Supplies: You'll need your slings from Activity 1, plastic golf balls or marshmallows, a tape measure, cardboard, markers, and a Bible.

Activity: Help your children use the cardboard to create a 9-foot tall Goliath cutout. You may want to attach the pieces of cardboard to a pile of empty boxes so the Goliath will be able to "stand" by himself. If not, simply attach the cardboard Goliath to a wall or hang it from the ceiling.

Share: When a man named Samuel was sent by God to find a new king, he considered many strong warriors. But none was chosen until a young boy, David, appeared before him. God told Samuel that David would be the new king—even though the other men were much stronger and more experienced. God did not look at the outward appearance, but at the heart.

Summarize the story of David and Goliath from 1 Samuel 17. Explain that Goliath (a huge Philistine warrior) had challenged the Israelites to send a champion to defeat him. If he could be defeated, the Philistine army would become their slaves. Tell how David refused to wear armor and instead, entered the battlefield with only a sling and a few stones, yet he still defeated Goliath.

? Have your children take turns standing next to the Goliath you've built. Then consider these questions:

• **How would you feel if you had to face a warrior as big as this?** (Scared; I wouldn't do it.)

Age Adjustments

OLDER CHILDREN struggle with self-esteem issues often. Use this story and activity as a springboard into discussion about how God cares for the person "inside" and is not concerned about how the outside appears. Explore together how that philosophy compares to the way older children feel about appearance. Help your children know that God loves them for who they are, not for the clothes they wear or because they have perfect teeth.

• **Why do you think David was confident when he faced Goliath?** (He knew God was on his side; he knew how to use a sling.)

 Have children take turns using the sling to hit your Goliath in the forehead, as David did. After a few tries, consider these questions:

• **What was it like to try and hit Goliath?** (We couldn't do it; we got one lucky shot.)

• **What does the story of David and Goliath tell us about how God chooses people for tasks?** (God chooses people because He knows what they can do; God didn't want a big warrior, He wanted David; God looks at the heart, not the outside.)

Close in prayer, thanking God for giving David the skill and confidence to face Goliath and asking God for that same confidence in your own life.

WRAP-UP

Gather everyone in a circle and have family members take turns answering this question: **What's one thing you've learned about God today?**

Next, tell kids you've got a new "Life Slogan" you'd like to share with them.

Life Slogan: Today's Life Slogan is this: "David killed Goliath with a little sling; with God you can do anything." Have family members repeat the slogan two or three times to help them learn it. Then encourage them to practice saying it during the week so they can talk about it at your next family night session.

Close in Prayer: Allow time for each family member to share prayer concerns and answers to prayer. Then close your time together with prayer for each concern. Thank God for listening to and caring about you.

Remember to record your prayer requests so you can refer to them in the future as you see God answering them.

Additional Resources:

David and Goliath Children's Discovery Bible action figures (ages 4-7)
Bible Greats David and Goliath playset (ages 4-10)
Veggie Tales® Playset: Dave and the Giant Pickle (ages 4-8)
Pocket Bible Stories: David and the Giant (ages 4-7)
Pencil Fun Books: David and the Giant Fighter (ages 4-7)

⊙ 11: Daniel

Exploring stories about Daniel

Scripture
• Daniel 5–6

ACTIVITY OVERVIEW		
Activity	Summary	Pre-Session Prep
Activity 1: Writing on the Wall	Use fingerpaint to write messages to each other and learn about how God used Daniel.	You'll need large sheets of paper or poster board, tape, fingerpaints, and a Bible.
Activity 2: In the Lions' Den	Create paper lions and play a game to learn how God protected Daniel.	You'll need paper, markers, scissors, and blindfolds.

Main Points:
　　—God uses many ways to get our attention.
　　—Obey God first.

LIFE SLOGAN: "Into the lions' den, Daniel trod; he was saved from harm by obeying God."

Make it your own

In the space provided below, outline the flow and add any additional ideas to guide you through the process of conducting this family night.

Prayer & Praise Items

In the space provided below, list any items you wish to pray about or give praise for during this family night session.

Journal

In the space provided below, capture a record of any fun or meaningful things which happened during this family night session.

Session Tip

We intentionally have provided more material than we would expect to be used in a single "Family Night" session. You know your family's unique interests and life circumstances best, so feel free to adapt this lesson to meet your family members' needs. Remember, short and simple is better than long and comprehensive.

 WARM-UP

Open with Prayer: Begin by having a family member pray, asking God to help everyone in the family understand more about Him through this time. After prayer, review your last lesson by asking these questions:

- **What did we learn about in our last lesson?**
- **What was the Life Slogan?**
- **Have your actions changed because of what we learned? If so, how?** Encourage family members to give specific examples of how they've applied learning from the past week.

Share: Today we're going to learn how God used Daniel and how He protected him from being eaten by hungry lions.

ACTIVITY 1: Writing on the Wall

Point: God uses many ways to get our attention.

Supplies: You'll need large sheets of paper or poster board, tape, fingerpaints, and a Bible.

Activity: Read or summarize the story of Daniel and King Belshazzar found in Daniel chapter 5. Here are a few key points to include:

- King Belshazzar did not honor God. He was disrespectful by drinking out of sacred gold and silver glasses at a big party. He also laughed at God.
- During the party, the fingers of a human hand appeared and wrote on the wall. The king watched and was frightened as the hands wrote: *Mene, Mene, Tekel, Upharsin.*
- The queen suggested King Belshazzar call on Daniel to interpret the strange words.

• Daniel came and explained that the words mean, "You will not be king much longer because you have not been a good king. Your enemies will take over your land."

Ask:

• **Why did God write on the wall during King Belshazzar's party?** (To get his attention; he wanted to tell the king something important.)

• **What are some ways we (parents) try to get your attention?** (Shouting at us when we're too close to the street; turning off the TV; saying you'll take us out for ice cream.)

Age Adjustments

OLDER CHILDREN can turn this activity into a fun guessing game. Have one child write a nonsense message or draw an unusual image to represent something God might be saying to them (for example, they might invent a code where numbers represent letters). Then have other family members attempt to interpret the message as Daniel did. If no one figures out the message, have the person who wrote it explain what it meant. Discuss how sometimes we have difficulty knowing what God is saying to us, and that the help of a friend, parent, or pastor can help to unravel the mystery.

Tape a large sheet of paper or poster board on a wall. To prevent spills from messing up your floor, you may want to do this activity in a garage or basement or you may simply want to place a drop cloth below the paper. And be sure to double check that the fingerpaints don't bleed through the paper! Have children each take a turn writing a message or drawing a picture of something God might be saying to them. For example, someone might write, "Obey your parents," or draw a picture of a heart to suggest that God wants us to love one another.

When everyone's had a turn drawing, share: **King Belshazzar made some bad choices in his life and God wanted to let him know He wasn't happy about that. God uses all kinds of creative ways to get our attention when we've done something wrong. But God doesn't get our attention just to make us feel bad—He wants us to learn what we're doing wrong so we can change and make things right.**

Pray together for God to show each family member the right things to do in life.

ACTIVITY 2: In the Lions' Den

Point: Obey God first.

 Supplies: You'll need paper, markers, scissors, and blindfolds.

Activity: Help your children create a dozen or so paper lions using the markers, paper, and scissors. Let your children decide how the lions should look, but make sure they're all at least 10 inches long (or 10 inches in diameter if you create just the lion's head). After decorating the lions, have one person place them randomly across the floor. Then blindfold family members and have them wander around the room attempting to avoid the paper lions. Periodically, move the lions around on the floor. It's likely that your children will step on a lion one or more times. If not, keep playing and moving the lions around until they do.

NOTE: This activity works best in a small room where there is little floor space to walk on that is not covered by one of the paper lions.

 Consider this question:

• **What was it like trying to avoid the lions?** (It wasn't easy; I couldn't do it; I almost did it.)

Share: In the time of King Darius, many people lost their lives as they were tossed into a lions' den. Just as we couldn't avoid the hungry lions on our floor, neither could those people avoid the real lions.

One day, King Darius told Daniel that he would put him in charge of all the kingdom. But two royal helpers overheard this and were jealous. They didn't want Daniel to be in charge. So they made a plan—they told King Darius he should make a law that it was wrong to pray. He agreed.

Age Adjustments

HELP OLDER CHILDREN explore times they've felt like Daniel in the lions' den. For example, they might feel the same way when their friends laugh at them because they admit to going to church or when they refuse to participate in bad behavior. Encourage your children to continue being confident in their faith, even when others challenge them or make fun of them.

Have family members imagine they're living in King Darius' time. Spend a few minutes in prayer, then **share: Because Daniel loved God very much, he didn't stop praying. And when he was caught, King Darius sadly had to send his friend Daniel into the lions' den. King Darius had been tricked by the royal helpers.**

Blindfold family members again and set them in your lions' den. Quietly collect the paper lions and set them in one corner of the room, far from family members. **Share: But when Daniel was sent to the lions' den, God shut the lions' mouths and Daniel was spared.**

Have everyone walk around the room, protecting them from the pile of lions as necessary. Then have everyone remove their blindfolds.

? Consider these questions:

- **What would you do if you knew you'd be thrown to the lions for praying?** (I'd stop praying; I'd pray silently; I'd pray anyway.)
- **Why did Daniel keep on praying?** (Because he knew it was right; God wanted him to.)
- **Why was Daniel saved from the lions?** (Because he obeyed God; because God loved him.)

Share: Though we may not always be saved from harm as Daniel was, the message of this Bible story is clear: obey God first. God wants us to follow Him always.

WRAP-UP

Gather everyone in a circle and have family members take turns answering this question: **What's one thing you've learned about God today?**

Next, tell kids you've got a new "Life Slogan" you'd like to share with them.

Life Slogan: Today's Life Slogan is this: "Into the lions' den, Daniel trod; he was saved from harm by obeying God." Have family members repeat the slogan two or three times to help them learn it. Then encourage them to practice saying it during the week so they can talk about it at your next family night session.

Close in Prayer: Allow time for each family member to share prayer concerns and answers to prayer. Then close your time together with prayer for each concern. Thank God for listening to and caring about us.

Remember to record your prayer requests so you can refer to them in the future as you see God answering them.

Additional Resources:

Pocket Bible Stories: Daniel and the Lions (ages 4-7)
Pencil Fun Books: In a Lions' Den (ages 4-7)

⊚ 12: Jonah

Exploring the story of Jonah and the big fish

Scripture
• Book of Jonah

ACTIVITY OVERVIEW		
Activity	Summary	Pre-Session Prep
Activity 1: Hide and Seek Jonah	Run away from responsibilities such as washing the dishes or cleaning up a room.	Supplies will vary.
Activity 2: In the Belly of the Fish	Create a huge "whale" and discuss how Jonah learned to obey God after running away from Him.	You'll need a fan, a large sheet of lightweight plastic, duct tape, and a flashlight.

Main Points:

—We can't hide from God.

—We should do what God wants even if we don't think we can.

LIFE SLOGAN: "From the belly of a fish, Jonah said one day; 'Deliver me, God, and I will obey.'"

Make it your own
In the space provided below, outline the flow and add any additional ideas to guide you through the process of conducting this family night.

Prayer & Praise Items
In the space provided below, list any items you wish to pray about or give praise for during this family night session.

Journal
In the space provided below, capture a record of any fun or meaningful things which happened during this family night session.

Session Tip

We intentionally have provided more material than we would expect to be used in a single "Family Night" session. You know your family's unique interests and life circumstances best, so feel free to adapt this lesson to meet your family members' needs. Remember, short and simple is better than long and comprehensive.

 WARM-UP

Open with Prayer: Begin by having a family member pray, asking God to help everyone in the family understand more about Him through this time. After prayer, review your last lesson by asking these questions:

- **What did we learn about in our last lesson?**
- **What was the Life Slogan?**
- **Have your actions changed because of what we learned? If so, how?** Encourage family members to give specific examples of how they've applied learning from the past week.

Share: Today we're going have fun exploring the story of Jonah and the big fish.

ACTIVITY 1: Hide and Seek Jonah

Point: We can't hide from God.

 **Supplies:** Supplies will vary.

Activity: Tell family members that the first part of this activity will be "chore time." Choose a variety of brief, age-appropriate responsibilities for each child and send them on their way to complete these. Here are a few ideas: pick up toys; feed pets; put their shoes in their closet; and so on. It's possible your children will balk at doing work for their family night—that's OK. You'll discuss their responses after the jobs are complete and the "I don't want to" attitude is one that will lead nicely into this activity. Make sure you do a few jobs too.

 When everyone is done, regroup for the following discussion:
- **What were your first thoughts when I asked you do to these jobs?** (I thought that it wouldn't be fun; I didn't want to do it; I wondered what you were thinking.)
- **How might your attitude have been different if God had**

spoken directly to you and asked you to do these things? (I still wouldn't have wanted to clean my room; I would have done them happily.)

Share: Many years ago, God asked a man named Jonah to do a very important thing. God wanted Jonah to go to a city called Nineveh and tell the people there that they were doing bad things. But Jonah didn't want to do that, so he got on a boat heading far away to try and run from God.

 Play a game of hide and seek with your family. Then ask:
- **How well could you hide during this game?** (Not very well, people found me right away; very well, no one could find me.)
- **Did God know where you were while you were hiding? Explain.** (Yes, God is everywhere; I think so, God is always near.)

Share: Jonah soon learned what we already know—you can't hide from God. No matter where we are, God is there with us. So God sent a storm to the boat where Jonah was trying to hide. When Jonah realized that the storm was God's way of telling him "you can't hide," he had the sailors throw him overboard to save them from the storm.

ACTIVITY 2: In the Belly of the Fish

Point: We should do what God wants even if we don't think we can.

Supplies: You'll need a powerful fan, a large sheet of lightweight black plastic, duct tape, and a flashlight.

Activity: In this activity, you'll be creating a huge "fish" you'll be able to sit inside. If you can't come up with the supplies to create the fish as described below, you can simply hang some blankets across a few chairs to create a "cave" that can serve as the belly of your fish. However, since this is such a fun event for your kids, it may be worth the extra effort to find the needed supplies.

Here's how to create the big fish. Spread out the large sheet of plastic on a floor where you'll be able to use the duct tape. Carefully tape along one side of the plastic to secure it to the floor. Then set a few chairs or other items under the plastic to determine the inside height of the big fish. Carefully tape the opposite side of the plastic and one end as well. Cut a couple small flaps in the end to allow air to flow through. Set your fan at the untaped end of the plastic and turn it on. Hold up the opening so the air blows into the plastic "cave." At this time, you may want to tape the front opening around the fan to make sure all of the air is blowing into the plastic. Leave enough space for entering and exiting the fish.

When your fish is ready, bring your family members into the room and climb inside (don't forget to bring a flashlight). Tell family members to imagine they're inside the belly of the fish as Jonah was after being tossed off the boat.

 Ask:

- **What's it like to be inside this big fish?** (I don't like it; it's kind of fun.)
- **What might Jonah have felt like as he sat in the fish for three days?** (Scared; confused; worried.)

Explain that while he was in the fish, Jonah thought about what God had asked him to do. Spend a little time talking about the things God wants your family members to do. This could be anything from "giving each other hugs" to "telling other people about God's love."

Then have the fish "spit" each family member out onto the "dry land." Turn off the fan and imagine the fish is slowly diving under the water.

Tell family members that Jonah did go to Nineveh and tell people what they were doing was wrong, as God had asked him in the first place. Share examples from your own life when God asked you to do something that was difficult. Then close in prayer, asking God to give each family member the strength to do what He asks of them.

Age Adjustments

OLDER CHILDREN may wonder if the message God gave Jonah might apply to them. Talk together about appropriate things they can do when they see their friends making bad decisions. This also might be a good opportunity to talk with your children about what it means to share their faith with friends.

YOUNGER CHILDREN may like to use sidewalk chalk and draw a big fish on the driveway. Then trace the whole family inside the fish, and tell the Jonah story. The kids love it.

WRAP-UP

Gather everyone in a circle and have family members take turns answering this question: **What's one thing you've learned about God today?**

Next, tell kids you've got a new "Life Slogan" you'd like to share with them.

Life Slogan: Today's Life Slogan is this: "From the belly of a fish, Jonah said one day; 'Deliver me, God, and I will obey.'" Have family members repeat the slogan two or three times to help them learn it. Then encourage them to practice saying it during the week so they can talk about it at your next family night session.

Close in Prayer: Allow time for each family member to share prayer concerns and answers to prayer. Then close your time together with prayer for each concern. Thank God for listening to and caring about us.

Remember to record your prayer requests so you can refer to them in the future as you see God answering them.

Additional Resources:

Pocket Bible Stories: Jonah and the Storm (ages 4-7)
Pencil Fun Books: Jonah's Fish Ride (ages 4-7)

@ How to Lead Your Child to Christ

SOME THINGS TO CONSIDER AHEAD OF TIME:

1. Realize that God is more concerned about your child's eternal destiny and happiness than you are. "The Lord is not slow in keeping His promise. . . . He is patient with you, not wanting anyone to perish, but everyone to come to repentance" (2 Peter 3:9).

2. Pray specifically beforehand that God will give you insights and wisdom in dealing with each child on his or her maturity level.

3. Don't use terms like "take Jesus into your heart," "dying and going to hell," and "accepting Christ as your personal Savior." Children are either too literal ("How does Jesus breathe in my heart?") or the words are too clichéd and trite for their understanding.

4. Deal with each child alone, and don't be in a hurry. Make sure he or she understands. Discuss. Take your time.

A FEW CAUTIONS:

1. When drawing children to Himself, Jesus said for others to "allow" them to come to Him (see Mark 10:14). Only with adults did He use the term "compel" (see Luke 14:23). Do not compel children.

2. Remember that unless the Holy Spirit is speaking to the child, there will be no genuine heart experience of regeneration. Parents, don't get caught up in the idea that Jesus will return the day before you were going to speak to your child about salvation and that it will be too late. Look at God's character—He *is* love! He is not dangling your child's soul over hell. Wait on God's timing.

    Pray with faith, believing. Be concerned, but don't push.

THE PLAN:

1. **God loves you.** Recite John 3:16 with your child's name in place of "the world."

2. **Show the child his or her need of a Savior.**

   a. Deal with sin carefully. There is one thing that cannot enter heaven—sin.

   b. Be sure your child knows what sin is. Ask him to name some (things common to children—lying, sassing, disobeying, etc.). Sin is doing or thinking anything wrong according to God's Word. It is breaking God's Law.

   c. Ask the question "Have you sinned?" If the answer is no, do not continue. Urge him to come and talk to you again when he does feel that he has sinned. Dismiss him. You may want to have prayer first, however, thanking God "for this young child who is willing to do what is right." Make it easy for him to talk to you again, but do not continue. Do not say, "Oh, yes, you have too sinned!" and then name some. With children, wait for God's conviction.

   d. If the answer is yes, continue. He may even give a personal illustration of some sin he has done recently or one that has bothered him.

   e. Tell him what God says about sin: We've all sinned ("There is no one righteous, not even one," Rom. 3:10). And because of that sin, we can't get to God ("For the wages of sin is death . . . " Rom. 6:23). So He had to come to us (". . . but the gift of God is eternal life in Christ Jesus our Lord," Rom. 6:23).

   f. Relate God's gift of salvation to Christmas gifts—we don't earn them or pay for them; we just accept them and are thankful for them.

3. **Bring the child to a definite decision.**

   a. Christ must be received if salvation is to be possessed.

   b. Remember, do not force a decision.

   c. Ask the child to pray out loud in her own words. Give her some things she could say if she seems unsure. Now be prepared for a blessing! (It is best to avoid having the child repeat a memorized prayer after you. Let her think, and make it personal.)*

d. After salvation has occurred, pray for her out loud. This is a good way to pronounce a blessing on her.

4. **Lead your child into assurance.**

Show him that he will have to keep his relationship open with God through repentance and forgiveness (just like with his family or friends), but that God will always love him ("Never will I leave you; never will I forsake you," Heb. 13:5).

* If you wish to guide your child through the prayer, here is some suggested language.

"Dear God, I know that I am a sinner [have child name specific sins he or she acknowledged earlier, such as lying, stealing, disobeying, etc.]. I know that Jesus died on the cross to pay for all my sins. I ask You to forgive me of my sins. I believe that Jesus died for me and rose from the dead, and I accept Him as my Savior. Thank You for loving me. In Jesus' name. Amen."

Cumulative Topical Index

TOPIC	SCRIPTURE	WHAT YOU'LL NEED	WHERE TO FIND IT
The Acts of the Sinful Nature and the Fruit of the Spirit	Gal. 5:19-26	3x5 cards or paper, markers, and tape	IFN, p. 43
Adding Value to Money through Saving Takes Time	Matt. 6:19-21	Supplies for making cookies and a Bible	MMK, p. 89
All Have Sinned	Rom. 3:23	Raw eggs, bucket of water	BCB, p. 89
All of Our Plans Should Match God's	Ps. 139:1-18	Paper, pencils, markers, or crayons	MMK, p. 73
Avoid Things That Keep Us from Growing	Eph. 4:14-15; Heb. 5:11-14	Seeds, plants at various stages of growth or a garden or nursery to tour, Bible	CCQ, p. 77
Bad Company Corrupts Good Character	1 Cor. 15:33	Small ball, string, slips of paper, pencil, yarn or masking tape, Bible	IFN, p. 103
Be Thankful for Good Friends		Bible, art supplies, markers	IFN, p. 98
Being Content with What We Have	Phil. 4:11-13	Bible	CCQ, p. 17
Being Diligent Means Working Hard and Well	Gen. 39–41	Bible, paper, a pencil and other supplies depending on jobs chosen	MMK, p. 64
Being a Faithful Steward Means Managing God's Gifts Wisely	1 Peter 4:10; Luke 19:12-26	Graham crackers, peanut butter, thin stick pretzels, small marshmallows, and M & Ms®	MMK, p. 18
Being Jealous Means Wanting Things Other People Have	Gen. 37:4-5	Different size boxes of candy or other treats, and a Bible	OTS, p. 39
Budgeting Means Making a Plan for Using Our Money	Jud. 6–7	Table, large sheets or paper, and markers or crayons	MMK, p. 79
Budgeting Means the Money Coming in Has to Equal the Money Going Out	Luke 14:28-35; Jud. 6–7	Supply of beans, paper, pencil, and Bible	MMK, p. 80

TOPIC	SCRIPTURE	WHAT YOU'LL NEED	WHERE TO FIND IT
Change Helps Us Grow and Mature	Rom. 8:28-39	Bible	WLS, p. 39
Change Is Good	1 Kings 17:8-16	Jar or box for holding change, colored paper, tape, markers, Bible	MMK, p. 27
Christ Is Who We Serve	Col. 3:23-24	Paper, scissors, pens	IFN, p. 50
Christians Should Be Joyful Each Day	James 3:22-23; Ps. 118:24	Small plastic bottle, cork to fit bottle opening, water, vinegar, paper towel, Bible	CCQ, p. 67
Commitment and Hard Work Are Needed to Finish Strong	Gen. 6:5-22	Jigsaw puzzle, Bible	CCQ, p. 83
The Consequence of Sin Is Death	Ps. 19:1-6	Dominoes	BCB, p. 57
Contentment Is the Secret to Happiness	Matt. 6:33	Package of candies, a Bible	MMK, p. 51
Creation	Gen. 1:1; Ps. 19:1-6; Rom. 1:20	Nature book or video, Bible	IFN, p. 17
David and Bathsheba	2 Sam. 11:1–12:14	Bible	BCB, p. 90
Description of Heaven	Rev. 21:3-4, 10-27	Bible, drawing supplies	BCB, p. 76
Difficulty Can Help Us Grow	Jer. 32:17; Luke 18:27	Bible, card game like Old Maid or Crazy Eights	CCQ, p. 33
Discipline and Training Make Us Stronger	Prov. 4:23	Narrow doorway, Bible	CCQ, p. 103
Don't Be Yoked with Unbelievers	2 Cor. 16:17–17:1	Milk, food coloring	IFN, p. 105
Don't Give Respect Based on Material Wealth	Eph. 6:1-8; 1 Peter 2:13-17; Ps. 119:17; James 2:1-2; 1 Tim. 4:12	Large sheet of paper, tape, a pen, Bible	IFN, p. 64
Easter Was God's Plan for Jesus	John 3:16; Rom. 3:23; 6:23	Paper and pencils or pens, materials to make a large cross, and a Bible	HFN, p. 27
Equality Does Not Mean Contentment	Matt. 20:1-16	Money or candy bars, tape recorder or radio, Bible	WLS, p. 21
Even if We're Not in the Majority, We May Be Right	2 Tim. 3:12-17	Piece of paper, pencil, water	CCQ, p. 95

AN INTRODUCTION TO FAMILY NIGHTS
= IFN

BASIC CHRISTIAN BELIEFS
= BCB

CHRISTIAN CHARACTER QUALITIES
= CCQ

WISDOM LIFE SKILLS
= WLS

MONEY MATTERS FOR KIDS
= MMK

HOLIDAYS FAMILY NIGHT
= HFN

BIBLE STORIES FOR PRESCHOOLERS (OLD TESTAMENT)
= OTS

TOPIC	SCRIPTURE	WHAT YOU'LL NEED	WHERE TO FIND IT
Every Day Is a Gift from God	Prov. 16:9	Bible	CCQ, p. 69
Evil Hearts Say Evil Words	Prov. 15:2-8; Luke 6:45; Eph. 4:29	Bible, small mirror	IFN, p. 79
Family Members Ought to Be Loyal to Each Other	The Book of Ruth	Shoebox, two pieces of different colored felt, seven pipe cleaners (preferably of different colors)	OTS, p. 67
The Fruit of the Spirit	Gal. 5:22-23; Luke 3:8; Acts 26:20	Blindfold and Bible	BCB, p. 92
God Allows Testing to Help Us Mature	James 1:2-4	Bible	BCB, p. 44
God Became a Man So We Could Understand His Love	John 14:9-10	A pet of some kind, and a Bible	HFN, p. 85
God Can Clean Our Guilty Consciences	1 John 1:9	Small dish of bleach, dark piece of material, Bible	WLS, p. 95
God Can Do the Impossible	John 6:1-14	Bible, sturdy plank (6 or more inches wide and 6 to 8 feet long), a brick or similar object, snack of fish and crackers	CCQ, p. 31
God Can Give Us Strength		Musical instruments (or pots and pans with wooden spoons) and a snack	OTS, p. 52
God Can Guide Us Away from Satan's Traps	Ps. 119:9-11; Prov. 3:5-6	Ten or more inexpensive mousetraps, pencil, blindfold, Bible	WLS, p. 72
God Can Help Us Knock Sin Out of Our Lives	Ps. 32:1-5; 1 John 1:9	Heavy drinking glass, pie tin, small slips of paper, pencils, large raw egg, cardboard tube from a roll of toilet paper, broom, masking tape, Bible	WLS, p. 53
God Can Use Us in Unique Ways to Accomplish His Plans		Strings of cloth, clothespins or strong tape, "glow sticks" or small flashlights	OTS, p. 63
God Cares for Us Even in Hard Times	Job 1–2; 42	Bible	WLS, p. 103
God Chose to Make Dads (or Moms) as a Picture of Himself	Gen. 1:26-27	Large sheets of paper, pencils, a bright light, a picture of your family, a Bible	HFN, p. 47

TOPIC	SCRIPTURE	WHAT YOU'LL NEED	WHERE TO FIND IT
God Created the Heavens and the Earth	Gen. 1	Small tent or sheet and a rope, Christmas lights, two buckets (one with water), a coffee can with dirt, a tape recorder and cassette, and a flashlight	OTS, p. 17
God Created Us	Isa. 45:9, 64:8; Ps. 139:13	Bible and video of potter with clay	BCB, p. 43
God Created the World, Stars, Plants, Animals, and People	Gen. 1	Play dough or clay, safe shaping or cutting tools, a Bible	OTS, p. 19
God Doesn't Want Us to Worry	Matt. 6:25-34; Phil. 4:6-7; Ps. 55:22	Bible, paper, pencils	CCQ, p. 39
God Forgives Those Who Confess Their Sins	1 John 1:9	Sheets of paper, tape, Bible	BCB, p. 58
God Gave Jesus a Message for Us	John 1:14,18; 8:19; 12:49-50	Goldfish in water or bug in jar, water	BCB, p. 66
God Gives and God Can Take Away	Luke 12:13-21	Bible, timer with bell or buzzer, large bowl of small candies, smaller bowl for each child	CCQ, p. 15
God Gives Us the Skills We Need to Do What He Asks of Us		Materials to make a sling (cloth, shoestrings), plastic golf balls or marshmallows, stuffed animals	OTS, p. 73
God Is Holy	Ex. 3:1-6	Masking tape, baby powder or corn starch, broom, Bible	IFN, p. 31
God Is Invisible, Powerful, and Real	John 1:18, 4:24; Luke 24:36-39	Balloons, balls, refrigerator magnets, Bible	IFN, p. 15
God Is the Source of Our Strength	Jud. 16	Oversized sweatshirt, balloons, mop heads or other items to use as wigs, items to stack to make pillars, a Bible	OTS, p. 61
God Is with Us	Ex. 25:10-22; Deut. 10:1-5; Josh. 3:14-17; 1 Sam. 3:3; 2 Sam. 6:12-15	A large cardboard box, two broom handles, a utility knife, strong tape, gold spray paint, and a Bible	OTS, p. 49
God Keeps His Promises	Gen. 9:13, 15	Sheets of colored cellophane, cardboard, scissors, tape, a Bible, a lamp or large flashlight	OTS, p. 25

TOPIC	SCRIPTURE	WHAT YOU'LL NEED	WHERE TO FIND IT
God Knew His Plans for Us	Jer. 29:11	Two puzzles and a Bible	BCB, p. 19
God Knew Moses Would Be Found by Pharaoh's Daughter	Ex. 2:1-10	A doll or stuffed animal, a basket, and a blanket	OTS, p. 43
God Knows All about Us	Ps. 139:2-4; Matt. 10:30	3x5 cards, a pen	BCB, p. 17
God Knows Everything	Isa. 40:13-14; Eph. 4:1-6	Bible	IFN, p. 15
God Knows the Plan for Our Lives	Rom. 8:28	Three different 25–50 piece jigsaw puzzles, Bible	WLS, p. 101
God Looks beyond the Mask and into Our Hearts		Costumes	HFN, p. 65
God Loves Us So Much, He Sent Jesus	John 3:16; Eph. 2:8-9	I.O.U. for each family member	IFN, p. 34
God Made Our Family Unique by Placing Each of Us in It		Different color paint for each family member, toothpicks or paintbrushes to dip into paint, white paper, Bible	BCB, p. 110
God Made Us		Building blocks, such as Tinkertoys, Legos, or K'nex	HFN, p. 15
God Made Us in His Image	Gen. 1:24-27	Play dough or clay and Bible	BCB, p. 24
God Never Changes	Ecc. 3:1-8; Heb. 13:8	Paper, pencils, Bible	WLS, p. 37
God Owns Everything; He Gives Us Things to Manage		Large sheet of poster board or newsprint and colored markers	MMK, p. 17
God Provides a Way Out of Temptation	1 Cor. 10:12-13; James 1:13-14; 4:7; 1 John 2:15-17	Bible	IFN, p. 88
God Sees Who We Really Are—We Can Never Fool Him	1 Sam. 16:7	Construction paper, scissors, crayons or markers, a hat or bowl, and a Bible	HFN, p. 66
God Teaches Us about Love through Others	1 Cor. 13	Colored paper, markers, crayons, scissors, tape or glue, and a Bible	HFN, p. 22
God Used Plagues to Tell Pharaoh to Let Moses and His People Go	Ex. 7–12	A clear glass, red food coloring, water, and a Bible	OTS, p. 44

TOPIC	SCRIPTURE	WHAT YOU'LL NEED	WHERE TO FIND IT
God Uses Many Ways to Get Our Attention	Dan. 5	Large sheets of paper or poster board, tape, finger-paint, and a Bible	OTS, p. 79
God Wants Our Best Effort in All We Do	Col. 3:23-24	Children's blocks or a large supply of cardboard boxes	MMK, p. 63
God Wants Us to Be Diligent in Our Work	Prov. 6:6-11; 1 Thes. 4:11-12	Video about ants or picture books or encyclopedia, Bible	CCQ, p. 55
God Wants Us to Get Closer to Him	James 4:8; 1 John 4:7-12	Hidden Bibles, clues to find them	BCB, p. 33
God Wants Us to Glorify Him	Ps. 24:1; Luke 12:13-21	Paper, pencils, Bible	WLS, p. 47
God Wants Us to Work and Be Helpful	2 Thes. 3:6-15	Several undone chores, Bible	CCQ, p. 53
God Will Send the Holy Spirit	John 14:23-26; 1 Cor. 2:12	Flashlights, small treats, Bible	IFN, p. 39
God's Covenant with Noah	Gen. 8:13-21; 9:8-17	Bible, paper, crayons or markers	BCB, p. 52
Guarding the Gate to Our Minds	Prov. 4:13; 2 Cor. 11:3; Phil. 4:8	Bible, poster board for each family member, old maga-zines, glue, scissors, markers	CCQ, p. 23
The Holy Spirit Helps Us	Eph. 1:17; John 14:15-17; Acts 1:1-11; Eph. 3:16-17; Rom. 8:26-27; 1 Cor. 2:11-16	Bible	BCB, p. 99
Honesty Means Being Sure We Tell the Truth and Are Fair	Prov. 10:9; 11:3; 12:5; 14:2; 28:13	A bunch of coins and a Bible	MMK, p. 58
Honor the Holy Spirit, Don't Block Him	1 John 4:4; 1 Cor. 6:19-20	Bible, blow-dryer or vacuum cleaner with exit hose, a Ping-Pong ball	CCQ, p. 47
Honor Your Parents	Ex. 20:12	Paper, pencil, treats, umbrella, soft objects, masking tape, pen, Bible	IFN, p. 55
How Big Is an Ark?		Large open area, buckets of water, cans of animal food, bags of dog food, and four flags	OTS, p. 24
If We Confess Our Sins, Jesus Will Forgive Us	Heb. 12:1; 1 John 1:9	Magic slate, candies, paper, pencils, bath-robe ties or soft rope, items to weigh some-one down, and a Bible	HFN, p. 28

TOPIC	SCRIPTURE	WHAT YOU'LL NEED	WHERE TO FIND IT
Investing and Saving Adds Value to Money	Prov. 21:20	Two and a half dollars for each family member	MMK, p. 87
It's Better to Follow the Truth	Rom. 1:25; Prov. 2:1-5	Second set of clues, box of candy or treats, Bible	WLS, p. 86
It's Better to Wait for Something Than to Borrow Money to Buy It	2 Kings 4:1-7; Prov. 22:7	Magazines, advertisements, paper, a pencil, Bible	MMK, p. 103
It's Difficult to Be a Giver When You're a Debtor		Pennies or other coins	MMK, p. 105
It's Easy to Follow a Lie, but It Leads to Disappointment		Clues as described in lesson, empty box	WLS, p. 85
The Importance of Your Name Being Written in the Book of Life	Rev. 20:11-15; 21:27	Bible, phone book, access to other books with family name	BCB, p. 74
It's Important to Listen to Jesus' Message		Bible	BCB, p. 68
Jesus Came to Die for Our Sins	Rom. 5:8	A large piece of cardboard, markers, scissors, tape, and a Bible	HFN, p. 91
Jesus Came to Give Us Eternal Life	Mark 16:12-14	A calculator, a calendar, a sheet of paper, and a pencil	HFN, p. 91
Jesus Came to Teach Us about God	John 1:14, 18	Winter clothing, bread crumbs, a Bible	HFN, p. 92
Jesus Came to Show Us How Much God Loves Us	John 3:16	Supplies to make an Advent wreath, and a Bible	HFN, p. 89
Jesus Died for Our Sins	Luke 22:1-6; Mark 14:12-26; Luke 22:47-54; Luke 22:55-62; Matt. 27:1-10; Matt. 27:11-31; Luke 23:26-34	Seven plastic eggs, slips of paper with Scripture verses, and a Bible	HFN, p. 33
Jesus Dies on the Cross	John 14:6	6-foot 2x4, 3-foot 2x4, hammers, nails, Bible	IFN, p. 33
Jesus Promises Us New Bodies and a New Home in Heaven	Phil. 3:20-21; Luke 24:36-43; Rev. 21:1-4	Ingredients for making pumpkin pie, and a Bible	HFN, p. 61

TOPIC	SCRIPTURE	WHAT YOU'LL NEED	WHERE TO FIND IT
Jesus Took Our Sins to the Cross and Freed Us from Being Bound Up in Sin	Rom. 6:23, 5:8; 6:18	Soft rope or heavy yarn, a watch with a second hand, thread, and a Bible	HFN, p. 53
Jesus Took the Punishment We Deserve	Rom. 6:23; John 3:16; Rom. 5:8-9	Bathrobe, list of bad deeds	IFN, p. 26
Jesus Was Victorious Over Death and Sin	Luke 23:35-43; Luke 23:44-53; Matt. 27:59-61; Luke 23:54–24:12	Five plastic eggs— four with Scripture verses, and a Bible	HFN, p. 36
Jesus Washes His Followers' Feet	John 13:1-17	Bucket of warm soapy water, towels, Bible	IFN, p. 63
Joshua and the Battle of Jericho	Josh. 1:16-18; 6:1-21	Paper, pencil, dots on paper that, when connected, form a star	IFN, p. 57
Knowing God's Word Helps Us Know What Stand to Take	2 Tim. 3:1-5	Current newspaper, Bible	CCQ, p. 93
Look to God, Not Others	Phil. 4:11-13	Magazines or news- papers, a chair, sev- eral pads of small yellow stickies, Bible	WLS, p. 24
Love Is Unselfish	1 Cor. 13	A snack and a Bible	HFN, p. 21
Loving Money Is Wrong	1 Tim. 6:6-10	Several rolls of coins, masking tape, Bible	WLS, p. 45
Lying Can Hurt People	Acts 5:1-11	Two pizza boxes— one empty and one with a fresh pizza— and a Bible	MMK, p. 57
Meeting Goals Requires Planning	Prov. 3:5-6	Paper, scissors, pen- cils, a treat, a Bible	MMK, p. 71
Moms Are Special and Important to Us and to God	Prov. 24:3-4	Confetti, streamers, a comfortable chair, a wash basin with warm water, two cloths, and a Bible	HFN, p. 41
Moms Model Jesus' Love When They Serve Gladly	2 Tim. 1:4-7	Various objects depending on chosen activity and a Bible	HFN, p. 42
The More We Know God, the More We Know His Voice	John 10:1-6	Bible	BCB, p. 35
Nicodemus Asks Jesus about Being Born Again	John 3:7, 50-51; 19:39-40	Bible, paper, pencil, costume	BCB, p. 81

AN INTRODUCTION TO FAMILY NIGHTS
= IFN

BASIC CHRISTIAN BELIEFS
= BCB

CHRISTIAN CHARACTER QUALITIES
= CCQ

WISDOM LIFE SKILLS
= WLS

MONEY MATTERS FOR KIDS
= MMK

HOLIDAYS FAMILY NIGHT
= HFN

BIBLE STORIES FOR PRESCHOOLERS (OLD TESTAMENT)
= OTS

AN
INTRODUCTION
TO FAMILY
NIGHTS
= IFN

BASIC
CHRISTIAN
BELIEFS
= BCB

CHRISTIAN
CHARACTER
QUALITIES
= CCQ

WISDOM LIFE
SKILLS
= WLS

MONEY
MATTERS FOR
KIDS
= MMK

HOLIDAYS
FAMILY NIGHT
= HFN

BIBLE STORIES
FOR
PRESCHOOLERS
(OLD TESTAMENT)
= OTS

TOPIC	SCRIPTURE	WHAT YOU'LL NEED	WHERE TO FIND IT
Noah Obeyed God When He Built the Ark	Gen. 6:14-16	A large refrigerator box, markers or paints, self-adhesive paper, stuffed animals, a Bible, utility knife	OTS, p. 23
Obedience Has Good Rewards		Planned outing everyone will enjoy, directions on 3x5 cards, number cards	IFN, p. 59
Obey God First		Paper, markers, scissors, and blindfolds	OTS, p. 80
Only a Relationship with God Can Fill Our Need	Isa. 55:1-2	Doll that requires batteries, batteries for the doll, dollar bill, pictures of a house, an expensive car, and a pretty woman or handsome man, Bible	WLS, p. 62
Our Conscience Helps Us Know Right from Wrong	Rom. 2:14-15	Foods with a strong smell, blindfold, Bible	WLS, p. 93
Our Minds Should Be Filled with Good, Not Evil	Phil 4:8; Ps. 119:9, 11	Bible, bucket of water, several large rocks	CCQ, p. 26
Parable of the Talents	Matt. 25:14-30	Bible	IFN, p. 73
Parable of the Vine and Branches	John 15:1-8	Tree branch, paper, pencils, Bible	IFN, p. 95
People Look at Outside Appearance, but God Looks at the Heart	1 Sam. 17	Slings from activity on p. 73, plastic golf balls or marshmallows, a tape measure, cardboard, markers, and a Bible	OTS, p. 75
Persecution Brings a Reward		Bucket, bag of ice, marker, one-dollar bill	WLS, p. 32
Planning Helps Us Finish Strong	Phil. 3:10-14	Flight map on p. 86, paper, pencils, Bible	CCQ, p. 85
Pray, Endure, and Be Glad When We're Persecuted	Matt. 5:11-12, 44; Rom. 12:14; 1 Cor. 4:12	Notes, Bible, candle or flashlight, dark small space	WLS, p. 29
Remember All God Has Done for You	Ex. 25:1; 16:34; Num. 17:10; Deut. 31:26	Ark of the covenant from p. 49, cardboard or Styrofoam, crackers, a stick, and a Bible	OTS, p. 51
Remember What God Has Done for You	Gen. 12:7-8; 13:18; 22:9	Bricks or large rocks, paint, and a Bible	OTS, p. 31

TOPIC	SCRIPTURE	WHAT YOU'LL NEED	WHERE TO FIND IT
The Responsibilities of Families	Eph. 5:22-33; 6:1-4	Photo albums, Bible	BCB, p. 101
Satan Looks for Ways to Trap Us	Luke 4:1-13	Cardboard box, string, stick, small ball, Bible	WLS, p. 69
Self-control Helps Us Resist the Enemy	1 Peter 5:8-9; 1 Peter 2:11-12	Blindfold, watch or timer, feather or other "tickly" item, Bible	CCQ, p. 101
Serve One Another in Love	Gal. 5:13	Bag of small candies, at least three per child	IFN, p. 47
Sin and Busyness Interfere with Our Prayers	Luke 10:38-42; Ps. 46:10; Matt. 5:23-24; 1 Peter 3:7	Bible, two paper cups, two paper clips, long length of fishing line	CCQ, p. 61
Sin Separates Humanity	Gen. 3:1-24	Bible, clay creations, piece of hardened clay or play dough	BCB, p. 25
Some Places Aren't Open to Everyone		Book or magazine with "knock-knock" jokes	BCB, p. 73
Some Things in Life Are Out of Our Control		Blindfolds	BCB, p. 41
Sometimes God Surprises Us with Great Things	Gen. 15:15	Large sheet of poster board, straight pins or straightened paper clips, a flashlight, and a Bible	OTS, p. 32
Sometimes We Face Things That Seem Impossible		Bunch of cardboard boxes or blocks	OTS, p. 55
Temptation Takes Our Eyes Off God		Fishing pole, items to catch, timer, Bible	IFN, p. 85
There Is a Difference between Needs and Wants	Prov. 31:16; Matt. 6:21	Paper, pencils, glasses of drinking water, a soft drink	MMK, p. 95
Those Who Don't Believe Are Foolish	Ps. 44:1	Ten small pieces of paper, pencil, Bible	IFN, p. 19
Tithing Means Giving One-Tenth Back to God	Gen. 28:10-22; Ps. 3:9-10	All family members need ten similar items each, a Bible	MMK, p. 33
The Tongue Is Small but Powerful	James 3:3-12	Video, news magazine or picture book showing devastation of fire, match, candle, Bible	IFN, p. 77
The Treasure of a Thankful Heart Is Contentment	Eph. 5:20	3x5 cards, pencils, fun prizes, and a Bible	HFN, p. 72

AN INTRODUCTION TO FAMILY NIGHTS
= IFN

BASIC CHRISTIAN BELIEFS
= BCB

CHRISTIAN CHARACTER QUALITIES
= CCQ

WISDOM LIFE SKILLS
= WLS

MONEY MATTERS FOR KIDS
= MMK

HOLIDAYS FAMILY NIGHT
= HFN

BIBLE STORIES FOR PRESCHOOLERS (OLD TESTAMENT)
= OTS

TOPIC	SCRIPTURE	WHAT YOU'LL NEED	WHERE TO FIND IT
Trials Help Us Grow	James 1:2-4	Sugar cookie dough, cookie cutters, baking sheets, miscellaneous baking supplies, Bible	WLS, p. 15
Trials Test How We've Grown	James 1:12	Bible	WLS, p. 17
Trust Is Important	Matt. 6:25-34	Each person needs an item he or she greatly values	MMK, p. 25
We All Sin	Rom. 3:23	Target and items to throw	IFN, p. 23
We Are a Family for Life, Forever	Ruth 1:4	Shoebox; scissors; paper or cloth; magnets; photos of family members, friends, others; and a Bible	OTS, p. 68
We Are Made in God's Image	Gen. 2:7; Ps. 139:13-16	Paper bags, candies, a Bible, supplies for making gingerbread cookies	HFN, p. 17
We Become a New Creation When Jesus Comes into Our Hearts	Matt. 23:25-28; Rev. 3:20; 2 Cor. 5:17; Eph. 2:10; 2 Cor. 4:7-10; Matt. 5:14-16; 2 Cor. 4:6	Pumpkin, newspaper, sharp knife, a spoon, a candle, matches, and a Bible	HFN, p. 59
We Can Communicate with Each Other			BCB, p. 65
We Can Fight the Temptation to Want More Stuff	Matt. 4:1-11; Heb. 13:5	Television, paper, a pencil, Bible	MMK, p. 49
We Can Give Joyfully to Others	Luke 10:25-37	Bible, soft yarn	MMK, p. 41
We Can Help Each Other	Prov. 27:17	Masking tape, bowl of unwrapped candies, rulers, yardsticks, or dowel rods	BCB, p. 110
We Can Help People When We Give Generously	2 Cor. 6–7	Variety of supplies, depending on chosen activity	MMK, p. 43
We Can Learn about God from Mom (or Dad)		Supplies to make a collage (magazines, paper, tape or glue, scissors)	HFN, p. 49
We Can Learn and Grow from Good and Bad Situations	Gen. 37–48; Rom. 8:29	A Bible and a camera (optional)	OTS, p. 37
We Can Love by Helping Those in Need	Heb. 13:1-3		IFN, p. 48

TOPIC	SCRIPTURE	WHAT YOU'LL NEED	WHERE TO FIND IT
We Can Show Love through Respecting Family Members		Paper and pen	IFN, p. 66
We Can't Hide from God		Supplies will vary	OTS, p. 85
We Can't Take Back the Damage of Our Words		Tube of toothpaste for each child, $10 bill	IFN, p. 78
We Deserve Punishment for Our Sins	Rom. 6:23	Dessert, other materials as decided	IFN, p. 24
We Give to God because We're Thankful		Supplies for a celebration dinner, also money for each family member	MMK, p. 36
We Have All We Need in Our Lives	Ecc. 3:11	Paper, pencils, Bible	WLS, p. 61
We Have a New Life in Christ	John 3:3; 2 Cor. 5:17	Video or picture book of caterpillar forming a cocoon then a butterfly, or a tadpole becoming a frog, or a seed becoming a plant	BCB, p. 93
We Have Much to Be Thankful For	1 Chron. 16:4-36	Unpopped popcorn, a bowl, supplies for popping popcorn, and a Bible	HFN, p. 79
We Know Others by Our Relationships with Them		Copies of question-naire, pencils, Bible	BCB, p. 31
We Must Be in Constant Contact with God		Blindfold	CCQ, p. 63
We Must Choose to Obey		3x5 cards or slips of paper, markers, and tape	IFN, p. 43
We Must Either Choose Christ or Reject Christ	Matt. 12:30	Clear glass jar, cooking oil, water, spoon, Bible	CCQ, p. 96
We Must Give Thanks in All Circumstances	1 Thes. 5:18	A typical family meal, cloth strips, and a Bible	HFN, p. 77
We Must Learn How Much Responsibility We Can Handle		Building blocks, watch with second hand, paper, pencil	IFN, p. 71
We Must Listen	Prov. 1:5, 8-9; 4:1	Bible, other supplies for the task you choose	WLS, p. 77
We Must Think Before We Speak	James 1:19	Bible	WLS, p. 79

Family Night
TOOL CHEST

AN INTRODUCTION TO FAMILY NIGHTS
= IFN

BASIC CHRISTIAN BELIEFS
= BCB

CHRISTIAN CHARACTER QUALITIES
= CCQ

WISDOM LIFE SKILLS
= WLS

MONEY MATTERS FOR KIDS
= MMK

HOLIDAYS FAMILY NIGHT
= HFN

BIBLE STORIES FOR PRESCHOOLERS (OLD TESTAMENT)
= OTS

TOPIC	SCRIPTURE	WHAT YOU'LL NEED	WHERE TO FIND IT
We Need to Grow Physically, Emotionally, and Spiritually	1 Peter 2:2	Photograph albums or videos of your children at different ages, tape measure, bathroom scale, Bible	CCQ, p. 75
We Prove Who We Are When What We Do Reflects What We Say	James 1:22; 2:14-27	A bag of candy, a rope, and a Bible	HFN, p. 67
We Reap What We Sow	Gal. 6:7	Candy bar, Bible	IFN, p. 55
We Should Do What God Wants Even If We Don't Think We Can		A powerful fan, large sheet of lightweight black plastic, duct tape, and a flashlight	OTS, p. 86
We Shouldn't Value Possessions Over Everything Else	1 Tim. 6:7-8	Box is optional	CCQ, p. 18
When God Sent Jesus to Earth, God Chose Me	Luke 1:26-38; John 3:16; Matt. 14:23	Going to choose a Christmas tree or other special decoration, a Bible, and hot chocolate	HFN, p. 83
When We Focus on What We Don't Have, We Get Unhappy	1 Tim. 6:9-10; 1 Thes. 5:18; Phil. 4:11-13	A glass, water, paper, crayons, and a Bible	HFN, p. 71
When We're Set Free from Sin, We Have the Freedom to Choose, and the Responsibility to Serve	Gal. 5:13-15	Candies, soft rope, and a Bible	HFN, p. 55
Wise Spending Means Getting Good Value for What We Buy	Luke 15:11-32	Money and a Bible	MMK, p. 97
With Help, Life Is a Lot Easier		Supplies to do the chore you choose	BCB, p. 101
Wolves in Sheeps' Clothing	Matt. 7:15-20	Ten paper sacks, a marker, ten small items, Bible	IFN, p. 97
Worrying Doesn't Change Anything		Board, inexpensive doorbell buzzer, a 9-volt battery, extra length of electrical wire, a large belt, assorted tools	CCQ, p. 37
You Look Like the Person in Whose Image You Are Created		Paper roll, crayons, markers, pictures of your kids and of yourself as a child	BCB, p. 23

Welcome to the Family!

Heritage Builders

Helping You Build a Family of Faith

We hope you've enjoyed this book. Heritage Builders was founded in 1995 by three fathers with a passion for the next generation. As a new ministry of Focus on the Family, Heritage Builders strives to equip, train and motivate parents to become intentional about building a strong spiritual heritage.

It's quite a challenge for busy parents to find ways to build a spiritual foundation for their families—especially in a way they enjoy and understand. Through activities and participation, children can learn biblical truth in a way they can understand, enjoy—and *remember.*

Passing along a heritage of Christian faith to your family is a parent's highest calling. Heritage Builders' goal is to encourage and empower you in this great mission with practical resources and inspiring ideas that really work— and help your children develop a lasting love for God.

***

How To Reach Us

For more information, visit our Heritage Builders Web site! Log on to **www.heritagebuilders.com** to discover new resources, sample activities, and ideas to help you pass on a spiritual heritage. To request any of these resources, simply call Focus on the Family at 1-800-A-FAMILY (1-800-232-6459) or in Canada, call 1-800-661-9800. Or send your request to Focus on the Family, Colorado Springs, CO 80995. In Canada, write Focus on the Family, P.O. Box 9800, Stn. Terminal, Vancouver, B.C. V6B 4G3

To learn more about Focus on the Family or to find out if there is an associate office in your country, please visit www. family.org

We'd love to hear from you!

Try These Heritage Builders Resources!

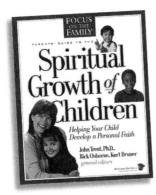

Parents' Guide to the
Spiritual Growth of Children

Building a foundation of faith in your children can be easy–
and fun!–with help from the *Parents' Guide to the Spiritual Growth
of Children*. Through simple and practical advice,
this comprehensive guide shows you how to build a
spiritual training plan for your family and it explains
what to teach your children at different ages.

Bedtime Blessings

Strengthen the precious bond between you, your child and God by making
Bedtime Blessings a special part of your evenings together. From best-selling author John
Trent, Ph.D., and Heritage Builders, this book is filled with stories, activities and blessing
prayers to help you practice the biblical model of "blessing."

My Time With God

Send your child on an amazing adventure—a self-guided tour through God's Word! *My Time
With God* shows your 8- to 12-year-old how to get to know God regularly in exciting ways.
Through 150 days' worth of fun facts and mind-boggling trivia, prayer starters, and
interesting questions, your child will discover how awesome God really is!

The Singing Bible

Children ages 2 to 7 will love *The Singing Bible*, which sets the Bible to music with over
50 fun, sing-along songs! Lead your child through Scripture by using *The Singing Bible*
to introduce the story of Jonah, the Ten Commandments and more.
This is a fun, fast-paced journey kids will remember.

· · ·

Visit our Heritage Builders Web Site! Log on to
www.heritagebuilders. com to discover new resources,
sample activities, and ideas to help you pass on a spiritual heritage.
To request any of these resources, simply call Focus on the Family at
1-800-A-FAMILY (1-800-232-6459) or in Canada, call 1-800-661-9800.
Or send your request to Focus on the Family, Colorado Springs, CO
80995. In Canada, Write Focus on the Family, P.O. Box 9800,
Stn. Terminal, Vancouver, B.C. V6B 4G3.

Heritage
Builders

Helping You Build a Family of Faith

Every family has a heritage—a spiritual, emotional, and social legacy passed from one generation to the next. There are four main areas we at Heritage Builders recommend parents consider as they plan to pass their faith to their children:

Family Fragrance

Every family's home has a fragrance. Heritage Builders encourages parents to create a home environment that fosters a sweet, Christ-centered AROMA of love through Affection, Respect, Order, Merriment, and Affirmation.

Family Traditions

Whether you pass down stories, beliefs and/or customs, traditions can help you establish a special identity for your family. Heritage Builders encourages parents to set special "milestones" for their children to help guide them and move them through their spiritual development.

Family Compass

Parents have the unique task of setting standards for normal, healthy living through their attitudes, actions and beliefs. Heritage Builders encourages parents to give their children the moral navigation tools they need to succeed on the roads of life.

Family Moments

Creating special, teachable moments with their children is one of a parent's most precious and sometimes, most difficult responsibilities. Heritage Builders encourages parents to capture little moments throughout the day to teach and impress values, beliefs, and biblical principles onto their children.

We look forward to standing alongside you as you seek to impart the Lord's care and wisdom onto the next generation—onto your children.

Heritage
Builders ™

Helping You Build a Family of Faith